APPROACHING GCSE ENGLISH

Pauline Paterson and Maureen Lloyd

The Authors:

Pauline Paterson and Maureen Lloyd are both teachers of English at the W.R. Tuson College, Preston. Between them they have many years' experience of teaching and examining at this level.

Editors:

Bren Abercrombie and Janet Day

Acknowledgements:

The authors particularly wish to thank:

David Eastham	Broughton High School
Joan Shaw	Ribbleton Hall High School
Margaret Woodrow	Kathryn Seed
	W.R. Tuson College Library Staff

and

Geoff Lloyd and David Paterson for all the photographs except those acknowledged at the back of the book.

The publishers wish to thank Pamela Ebdon for her assistance.

First published 1985 by

Framework Press
St. Leonard's House
St. Leonardgate
Lancaster LA1 1NN

Approaching GCSE English

© 1985 P. Paterson and M. Lloyd

ISBN 1 85008 035 6

Cover Design by John Angus

Illustrations by Christopher Stephens

Typeset by Blackpool Typesetting
Services Ltd

Printed & bound in Great Britain by
Redwood Burn Limited, Trowbridge, Wiltshire
Reprinted March 1986
2nd Reprint June 1986
3rd Reprint September 1986
4th Reprint January 1987
5th Reprint July 1987
6th Reprint August 1987

For
David, Katharine, Helen
my parents and Kath.

For
Geoff, Catherine, Michael,
my parents and parents-in-law.

TABLE OF CONTENTS

INTRODUCTION

PART A of this book contains general advice on some of the principal skills required for the three elements—writing, reading and oral communication—of GCSE English. PART B consists of original material which is intended to provide practice in writing and reading skills. The practice material has been arranged to reflect the general pattern of existing GCSE/16+ English examination questions and much of it is intended to be suitable for course work.

The material we have devised is intended to fulfil the objectives outlined in the GCSE National Criteria for English, March 1985. Thus, we have sought to provide opportunities for pupils to practise their ability to:

"—understand and convey information

—understand, order and present facts, ideas and opinions

—evaluate information in reading material and in other media, and select what is relevant to specific purposes

—articulate experience and express what is felt and what is imagined

—recognise implicit meaning and attitudes

—show a sense of audience and an awareness of style in both formal and informal situations

—exercise control of appropriate grammatical structures, conventions of paragraphing, sentence structure, punctuation and spelling in their writing

—communicate effectively and appropriately in spoken English."

Since GCSE syllabuses vary considerably, we have tried to take account of these differences in the book. We must draw our readers' attention, however, to the absolute necessity of consulting their particular syllabus to check its precise requirements. We have referred to our student readers throughout as candidates and where, in Part A, Chapter Three—Spoken English, we speak of the examiner, we do, of course, mean the student's own teacher acting in the capacity of an examiner.

We hope both students and teachers find the material in this book as useful as it was intended to be.

PART A

EXPRESSION

In this chapter we shall look at the part of the examination which requires you to produce continuous pieces of writing and at the different skills you will be expected to demonstrate. You may be asked to produce writing which is formal or personal, factual or imaginative. This, along with the time available, the length of the piece and the marks allocated to it, will vary according to your examination board.

How many pieces of continuous writing will be required?

Generally, TWO in an examination and TEN if you are producing a folio of course work. You should, of course, check your syllabus for the exact number.

We shall be considering the following forms of written expression:

1. The essay

2. The article

3. The letter

4. The report

5. The speech

6. The review

7. The short story

8. The description

9. The account of personal experience

For each form of writing we shall give:

(a) general advice on how to tackle it

and

(b) one sample question.

Then we shall supply you with

(c) all or part of an answer to the question, done by a student, accompanied by a few, brief comments from us. We must stress that these pieces of work are **NOT** model answers. They have been included because we hope you will find them a useful basis for discussion of the kinds of writing they represent.

In addition we shall include, wherever it seems likely to be helpful to you:

(d) advice based on examiners' reports. This advice will be printed inside a box, so that your attention is drawn to it.

Before we look more closely at the nine kinds of continuous writing which may be required on GCSE examination papers, let us consider three crucial aspects of *all* continuous writing: content, organisation and mechanical accuracy.

A. **Content** is the material you use to answer the question. It sounds simple, doesn't it? Yet every year significant numbers of candidates do not do as well in examinations as they had hoped, because the content of their answers was not entirely *RELEVANT* to the questions: *They had not really answered the questions*. This danger is particularly prevalent where a great deal of stimulus material is supplied in the question.

What happens if your material is irrelevant?

You may lose a couple of marks—or you may be marked down by one or two grades. So be very careful. Read the question more than once. Underline or itemize exactly what you have to do and bear that in mind throughout your answer.

Length is rarely stipulated on examination papers, but as a general guide your pieces of continuous writing should be about 400—500 words long. Answers which are shorter than this may well be penalised because they are inadequate. Some candidates—often weaker ones— write too much. It does not do them any good. They make more and more errors and tend to repeat themselves.

A writer's *style* is, of course, a very personal matter but, for examination purposes, it is as well to:

—express yourself in as clear and straightforward a way as you can.

—try to vary the length and complexity of your sentences.

—be a little more adventurous in your choice of vocabulary than you would be in ordinary speech.

—use figures of speech occasionally—wherever they seem appropriate.

—avoid colloquialisms and slang, except in the *rare* cases when more formal language would be unconvincing in the context.

...nt in your answer
...ry grade. Often, in
...a lot of stimulus
...to the candidate, a
...on's various require-
...*directions, watch out,*
...If, for instance, you
...ews on an issue, you
...*ons* for thinking as you
...

Baljit: 'I see the examiner as a powerful person; he has power over us and the whole education system.'

Sometimes examination questions are very short and capable of a variety of interpretations. Your answer may be indecisive and disorganised because you are unsure about what the question is asking you to do. In this case, it is best to *choose an obvious, straightforward interpretation of the question, limit the scope of your answer but go into the subject in some depth.* Take, as an example, an examination question which consists of just two words, 'Coming home'. One way of tackling this would be to describe several different aspects of what coming home means to one person. That could be the basis of your plan. What you must avoid, however, is writing at length about what happened to the person *before* he or she came home, without

making it clear throughout your answer that 'Coming home' is your *central* theme. The point is that where a question permits a variety of interpretations, you must ensure that your inter- pretation is entirely *relevant*.

Usually, continuous writing of 400–500 words should be organised into *five or six fairly lengthy paragraphs*, each on a different aspect of the subject-matter. Certain types of writing, short stories, for instance, will not fall easily into this pattern—and, of course, there is no reason why they should.

> Just remember, however, that a series of very short paragraphs or a complete lack of paragraphs is to be avoided. The first is frequently taken as an indication that the candidate is unable to develop his ideas, and the second that he is unable to organise them.

C. **Mechanical accuracy** in your writing is essential if you are to achieve a better-than-average mark for it. This means that ideally your writing should not contain any errors of spelling, punctuation or grammar. You may feel that, for you, this is an impossibility. Do not despair. How many of us can be totally accurate when we are writing at speed, as we usually are in examinations? But we can all increase our *level* of accuracy with a little effort.

> If we concentrate on eradicating our most frequent mistakes . . . If, perhaps, we could learn how to write sentences . . . If, possibly, we could learn when to use full-stops and when to use commas . . . Humour aside, the ability to write in sentences is crucial to success in the examination.

Your syllabus may permit you to use a diction- ary. If you acquire the habit of using one effici- ently, it will help you to produce work in which the spelling is accurate and the vocabulary appro- priate. Unfortunately, a dictionary is not a great deal of help if your spelling is very weak. The best remedy here is to find the correct versions of the words you most frequently mis-spell—and to *learn* them!

1. The Essay

In many of the essay questions which require a discursive treatment, a lot of information is provided for the candidate. This information may be presented in a variety of ways, such as:

Extracts from newspapers and magazines

Reports

Notes

Statistical tables

Maps and diagrams

Drawings and photographs

Letters

Other people's opinions

and may well consist of a combination of two or three of these.

There are two important points to note about these questions:

(i) You are asked to discuss and refer to *some* of the information but you *need not refer to it all*. This is because there is frequently too much information for you to deal satisfactorily with it all and because the examiner is looking for ideas which are *developed*, based upon selected material. If the question requires it, the examiner may also ask you to *compare* or to *contrast material*.

(ii) In addition to the information which is supplied, you need *your own ideas*. You are expected to select from the material available, to link sections of it together, where appropriate, and from it to develop your own ideas.

> Candidates who try to use all the information are, generally, the weaker ones because they find it very hard to write on a sustained theme for a paragraph or so. Instead they mistakenly try to cover the ground by making one comment about one item of information and then another, single comment about a further piece of information, and so on. Such candidates tend to score only a low grade.

> The weakest candidates waste time copying out whole paragraphs of information, instead of making use of short quotations from them or referring to them briefly, to support their argument. Others regurgitate the information on the examination paper in their own words, evidently believing that they are answering the question, when, of course, they have not even begun to do so.
>
> *The best candidates are those who can sustain a point of view or an argument by using the stimulus material in conjunction with their own general knowledge.*

Example

THE NUCLEAR ISSUE

Study the comments below and then discuss some of the points they raise, adding points of your own in order to develop your argument. You need not refer to all the points.

Cabinet Minister

'It is fifty years since there was a war in Europe. This is due in large measure to the deterrent effect of nuclear weapons.'

World Disarmament Campaign leaflet

'In December, 1982 the U.N. General Assembly voted overwhelmingly (112 to 16) for an immediate freeze on the production and deployment of new nuclear weapons by the nuclear-weapon states. The 16 who voted against included the United Kingdom.'

Shipyard Worker

'How can we trust the Russians? They have military superiority, don't they? If we gave up our nuclear weapons, there would be nothing to stop them invading us. Anyway, building nuclear submarines is how I earn my living!'

Nikita Kruschev

'In the event of a nuclear war the living would envy the dead'.

Charity Relief Worker

'It is morally wrong to spend enormous amounts of money on the arms race when half the world's population live in hopeless poverty. Fifty million children could be adequately fed for the cost of just one American MX missile.'

Spokesman for Ministry of Defence

'Britain is the most vulnerable nuclear target in the world with its combination of a high population density and multiple military installations close to the centres of population. Trident, therefore, is essential to our security.'

Member of Parliament

'Civil Defence measures can provide security for at least a large part of the population. Sweden and Switzerland have built underground shelters for millions of people. Britain should do the same.'

Research Scientist

'In a Britain devastated by nuclear war, the survivors, many of them severely injured by the blast and by radiation, would face a world of freezing darkness.'

THE NUCLEAR ISSUE

Which points does Tim use from the original question?

How does he develop **his** ideas based on these points?

I believe that all war is wrong. The build up in the arms race makes man more vulnerable and war more likely. I think that Britain ought to make a lead and disarm — perhaps it will only take one country's lead and the rest will follow.

The Cabinet Minister claims that the peace since World War II has been due to the presence of nuclear weapons. I accept that they may have had a short term stabilising effect, but this does not mean that they are right or that they will bring long term peace. There have however regularly been wars in the rest of the world. I accept that Britain must have a form of defence, but a conventional one not a nuclear one. Surely the danger at the moment from Eastern Europe exists not from nuclear weapons but from conventional or germ warfare. If we therefore run down our conventional weapons we are allowing Britain to face the threat of invasion.

Look at the references to the originators of these comments and consider other possible ways of introducing them.

I totally disagree with the Ministry of Defence Spokesman - the U.S.S.R. would never bomb us with nuclear weapons because we are too close to them and they would risk a nuclear winter and depending on the direction of the wind, radiation. Britain is far more vulnerable with nuclear weapons for they lull us into a false sense of security. If the U.S.S.R attempted to invade with conventional weapons they might succeed and no one would dare fight them with nuclear weapons. Therefore Western Europe will be in constant danger unless they disarm and start concentrating on building a defence based on soldiers, aircraft, tanks etc. This kind of war is also morally wrong, but does not endanger the future of the world.

The shipyard worker has a totally wrong attitude about his job. If Britain's government decided to stop building submarines etc. then they could transfer the factors of production to the manufacture of some other good. I agree with the Charity Relief worker's view and it is also true that the money spent on nuclear weapons in a fortnight would be enough to feed, house and educate everyone on the earth, where 2/3 of the population regularly go hungry. The shipyard worker could be re-trained so that he could participate in the production of a good which provides genuine benefit for millions of starving people. After all what is the purpose of making enough nuclear weapons to blow the world up several times over?

The M.P. says that we ought to build shelters. This is a strange view because the effects of nuclear war could last for years and as Nickita Kruschev says, the survivors (even underground) would envy the dead. Also a problem of this is we cannot produce protection for only part of the population. How would we decide who is to live and who is to die as in God's eyes everyone is equal. - even the tramp in Glasgow is as good as Mrs. Thatcher - and it is not for man to judge who is better.

Can you see where he links together two points taken from the source material?

How does Tim deal with writers he disagrees with?

In my opinion the danger of nuclear war comes not from the superpowers, but from other parts of the world. Imagine the dangers if a man like Colonel Gadaffi was to gain them. If he became enraged with someone he would have no qualms about using a nuclear weapon, as long as he could disappear into his shelter when the other side retaliated. The greatest chance of one of the superpowers of letting off a nuclear bomb would be by accident. A number of such accidents have already occurred, but fortunately without major disaster.

I believe therefore that we ought to disarm and transfer the resources to producing goods which produce wealth for all mankind.

Tim Mansfield.

2. The Article

An article needs:

(i) *an eye-catching headline*, which may include a pun, an abbreviation or an ambiguity.

(ii) an opening, *a key sentence*, which is, in effect, a summary or statement of the main theme of the article and which will often contain the essential facts. It is rather like putting the conclusion of an essay first; once you have stated it, you start again at the beginning of your information and work your way through to the end. After the key sentence, therefore, you need:

(iii) *additional paragraphs*, providing facts and ideas which develop and explain all aspects of the key sentence. The paragraphs in newspaper and magazine articles tend to consist of one or two sentences, but your paragraphs should, in the main, consist of several sentences. You may like to introduce one or two of them with a brief sub-heading, perhaps a word or phrase lifted from the paragraphs themselves.

(iv) *quotations* from witnesses/victims/experts or other interviewees may also be appropriate. It is usual to mention each interviewee's name as well as other pertinent details such as age, address and occupation.

In your article, you should aim to produce a well-organised, logical piece of writing, in which all the aspects of the key sentence have been explored in a clear and factual style.

Example

ZOOS

The comments printed below are concerned with zoos. Read them carefully and then, by discussing some of the points they raise, write an article on zoos and their future. You do not have to refer to all the points made below and you may, of course, add information of your own.

Zoo Director

'The hey-day of zoos came in the late 1950s and early 1960s. Ever since then, unfortunately, costs have risen sharply, whilst attendances have declined.'

Member of the Ratepayers' Association

'Why should we subsidise our local zoo to the tune of £250,000 a year, when essential services for the young and the elderly are being cut because of lack of money?'

Mother of Two

'I can't understand why zoos can't pay their way. They have hundreds of thousands of visitors a year at most zoos. It makes a lovely day out for the family.'

13 Year Old Boy

'There's nothing special about visiting a zoo. I'd rather play a space invaders machine.'

Teacher

'A visit to a zoo for city children such as mine has great educational value. Whatever they cost to run, zoos are worth it for what they can teach us about the wonders of nature.'

16 Year Old Girl

'Do we really need zoos at all? What function do they serve? The poor animals are kept in confined spaces, sometimes without companionship, just so that ignorant human beings can go and stare at them as if they were freaks. I don't agree with zoos at all. I much prefer safari parks because there, at least, the animals have a lot more space.'

Have Animals Lost Their Magic?

How is
the source
material
introduced
here?

More and more British zoos are finding it difficult to make ends meet according to Jonathan Matthews, Director of Ridgeway Zoo. Rising costs and declining attendance figures are threatening the zoo's future and local ratepayers face a bill of £250,000 annually if the zoo is to be kept open.

Entertainment

How much of
this
information
has Gary
himself
supplied?

In England, zoos began with William I's 'menagerie' at Woodstock. Historically, most zoos were started simply for private or public entertainment and only a fraction were begun to promote serious scientific experiment. In Britain in 1945, fourteen zoos existed and this total was doubled within a few years. The hey-day of zoos came in the late 1950's and early 1960's when people of the working classes had greater spending power with more to spend.

Novelty Gone

In what way
does Gary
make use of
the source
material
here?

The novelty of zoos even with the introduction of more and different species has gradually tended to diminish. This backs up the view that kids today would rather play on Space Invaders than visit a "boring old zoo". Times have obviously changed since the 1950's and 1960's and new ideas have been introduced in the form of leisure. During the past few years, the morals of keeping animals locked up has constantly come under criticism from animal rights groups and other believers like them. This may have added to the decreased attendances lately.

Gary Hardacre

This is just
the first
page of a
longer piece
of work.

3. The Letter

If you are invited to write a letter, check the instructions in the question thoroughly to determine whether an informal/personal letter is required or whether it is to assume a formal/business format. Look at the question, too, to see how long the letter should be. The question may state the length of the body of the letter, that is, the main section of the letter *minus* the address(es), the date, the salutation and the subscription. Where no specific length is given, assume that the body of the letter is to be as long as an essay, that is, between 400 and 500 words.

(i) **An informal/personal letter** is set out like this:

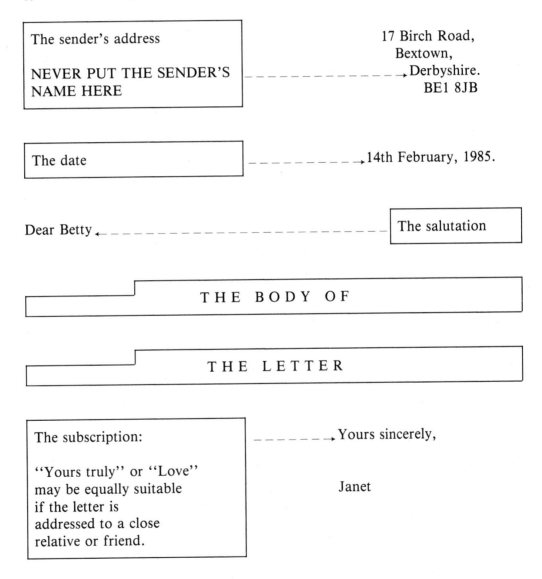

(ii) **A formal/business letter** may be set out like this:

| The sender's address | - - - - - - - - - - - - - → | 32 Oak Crescent,
Ashton.
AN3 7DP |

| The date | - - - - - - - - - - - - - → | 14th February, 1985. |

The Editor,
"Ashton Courier", ← - - - - - - - - - - Name or title of recipient and recipient's address
High Street,
Ashton.
AN1 6KF

Dear Sir, ← - - - - - - - - - - The salutation: Use the name of the recipient. If the title only is known, use "Dear Sir". If neither name nor title are known, when writing to a firm, use "Dear Sirs".

THE   BODY   OF

THE   LETTER

The subscription:
End with "Yours faithfully"
if you began with "Dear Sir"
or "Dear Sirs". End with
"Yours sincerely" if you
began with the recipient's name.   - - - - - → Yours faithfully,

Janet Smith

Note

1. Avoid using abbreviations in the address(es) and the date. (After all, you are trying to score a good mark, so make an effort to please the examiner's eye.)

2. Avoid, also, beginning a letter with "I am writing . . .". In a letter to the editor of a newspaper, for instance, a more realistic and effective start might be along these lines -

'Your correspondent, John Brown, (Ashton Courier, 14th February, 1985) presented a very limited case for arming the police. Has he considered how this might affect the numbers of violent crimes? . . .'

Example

SOCCER VIOLENCE

Read the extract below, from an article which appeared in "The Daily Reporter" on March 22nd, 1985.

Write a letter to the editor giving your views on this incident and your conclusions on soccer violence in general.

The body of the letter should be not less than 18 lines of average size writing and it should be properly set out. Write appropriately and organise your material well. In this question the main emphasis is on clear, concise and logical explanation.

Soccer Riot City Counts the Cost

from John Hancock in Barcelona

A shocked city was yesterday counting the cost of one of Europe's worst nights of soccer violence.

Damage caused by Castletown Rangers fans rampaging through the streets of Barcelona is estimated at £250,000 to £500,000. But the cost of trying to maintain law and order at the match with Barcelona on Wednesday night will put the final figure much higher.

Eight hundred police officers were on duty, along with 150 Red Cross volunteers and paramedics.

The Prime Minister apologised to Spain for the behaviour of the Rangers fans.

She told M.P.s: 'We are all deeply concerned about the violence displayed in Barcelona and would totally and utterly condemn it.'

'It was a disgrace to Britain and we deeply apologise for it.'

During the violence, one Rangers fan was knifed to death and two others received gunshot wounds.

The dead Rangers fan, Trevor Burke, 20, of Railway Street, Castletown, was knifed during a fight in a bar. Peter Jackson, 19, and Raymond Finney, 24, also of Castletown, were treated in hospital for gunshot wounds to the legs.

Of about 200 Rangers fans arrested on Wednesday, all but six have been released. They will be charged with criminal damage and grievous bodily harm.

The Yew Trees,
Whiteleo Lane,
Chorley,
Lancashire.

The Editor,
The 'Daily Reporter' Newspaper,
172, High Street,
PRESTON,
Lancashire.

March 24th, 1985.

Dear Sir,

What is commendable about this opening sentence and what might be improved?

I have read your article on the recent behaviour of Castletown Rangers' Fans in Barcelona, in the 'Daily Reporter' Newspaper of March 22nd, 1985. I feel that I must express my views on this latest incident of football hooliganism which brings shame to Britain.

I am convinced that if the cost of damage caused by fans, which was estimated at around half a million pounds, was paid for by the football clubs whose fans were involved along with the fans themselves then the clubs in future would vet their applicants for tickets to away matches abroad more carefully. In the case of the fan knifed to death a proper murder inquiry should take place to find the killer who in turn should be tried and prosecuted. All weapons and alcohol should be banned from matches and fans should be searched before entering the stadium.

If this sentence were broken up with two or three shorter ones, how might this be done? Would it be an improvement?

What aspects of the article did Susanne choose to comment on?

What might she have commented on?

Finally, if this type of violence continues at football matches then I believe the Prime Minister should do more than merely 'condemn' the behaviour. She should suggest that fans are not allowed at football matches abroad and that in fact the game is televised instead. This would save money, lives and the reputation of our country.

Yours faithfully,

Susanne R. Illsley (Miss).

4. The Report and Formal Statement

Reports vary considerably. At the one end of the scale is the elaborate and costly report like those issued by committees set up by the government; at the other, is the simple report which has to be completed by someone as part of his routine work. Generally, the kind of report you are likely to have to write needs:

(i) *a title*, usually in the form of "A Report on . . .". You may include the name and title of the recipient here whilst the date and name of the writer will normally go at the end of the report.

(ii) *terms of reference*, which supply the background to the report in brief, that is the circumstances or happenings which have made it necessary, and which state its objective or purpose. Next, if it is appropriate to the particular question you have been set, comes

(iii) *the procedure*, that is, the way you find your information. This is followed by

(iv) *the findings*, that is, the facts or evidence. If you are writing a report as a piece of course work, your sources of information may consist of printed material, or oral evidence, or may result from a practical examination of the situation. Alternatively, if a report is asked for on an examination paper, and no facts are given upon which to write it, make up some plausible facts, based, as far as possible, on your own experience. Present the facts in an ordered, logical way and include only material which is relevant. Then give your

(v) *conclusions*, which should follow logically from the facts. Sometimes you may be invited to supply your

(vi) *recommendations* which will usually consist of practical suggestions based on your conclusions.

Apart from a report, you may be asked to write what amounts to a formal statement such as that which might be given by someone either involved in, or witness to, some kind of incident. In this case, the facts/the evidence and your conclusions are the most important features.

After you have read this sample question, you can see how one of our students tackled it.

Sample REPORT

CHIPS WITH EVERYTHING

Study the notes below, which are based on the findings of research into the eating habits of secondary school children. By using some of this material and additional information of your own, write a report on school children's diets for your local education committee, who are keen to hear the views of children themselves. Discuss possible causes of unbalanced diets, draw your conclusions and make your recommendations as to how school children may be encouraged to eat a healthy diet.

(a) Well over half the secondary school children in the survey had chips at lunchtime every day.

(b) High fat content in food is one of the chief causes of coronary heart disease, now well-established as the biggest killer in the western world. Children who eat large amounts of fatty food may predispose themselves to the disease in adult life.

(c) According to one of the catering supervisors interviewed in the survey, not many children will buy a school meal when chips are not on the menu.

(d) Attempts by school meals staff to introduce children to a healthier diet have been only partially successful. Many still request chips with salad, for instance.

(e) School tuck shops add to the problem by selling large quantities of crisps and other fried snacks, which have approximately a 70% fat content.

(f) Under the cafeteria system, in operation in many secondary schools, pupils are left to select food unsupervised. Money-conscious pupils are able to pocket most of their dinner money and opt for a stodgy snack; figure-conscious pupils are able to settle for just a drink for their lunch.

(g) Food served in school cafeterias should be colour coded to show both fat and protein content.

(h) School children should be educated about the dangers associated with an unhealthy diet.

A Report on the Diets of schoolchildren at Longwood High School.

Terms of Reference.

The members of the Longwood Education Committee are very concerned that schoolchildren are eating too much fatty food. Fatty food is one of the main causes of heart disease and children who eat too much of it may endanger their health in later life. The education committee would like to find out more about what children eat during school hours and they have asked for a report on school-children's diets from a number of schools.

Procedure.

To find out what I wanted to know, I talked to my friends and used my own observations of what happens at lunchtime in my school.

By what other methods might Jo Ann have obtained her information?

Findings.

At my school about three quarters of the children have chips at lunchtime, the boys probably more than the girls. While salads are available every day, there are a lot of foods on the menu which contain a lot of fat. Apart from chips we can choose from meals such as steak puddings, meat and potato pies, fruit pies and cream, Manchester tart and so on. In winter many children prefer hot, filling food such as chips and beans or chips and sausage. It is certainly the case at my school that when chips are not on the menu a lot of pupils visit the local chippy instead of having a school dinner. Girls will eat salads but not many of the boys seem to like them. When they do choose salad, they often have chips as well. and put salad cream on their chips. This adds to the number of calories.

Consider the ways in which Jo Ann refers to the source material.

Our tuck shop doesn't sell sweets or chocolates, just crisps. Some crisps are cooked in vegetable oil which isn't harmful as animal fat. When I was in the first year we had a dinner ticket

Are there any points in the source material which are not discussed in the report?

System; we exchanged a ticket for one main course and one sweet from a choice of two or three. There wasn't as much choice as under the cafeteria system but at least you were getting a proper, reasonably balanced meal. It's true to say that some lads as well as some girls will buy a plate of chips for there dinner so that they can keep some of their money to buy cigarettes with.

From about the age of twelve onwards, girls became figure concious and want to be very slim so that they can wear the latest fashions. I remember when I was that age, My friend and I used to eat salads at school. We decided we wouldn't eat potatoes or anything fattening. One girl whose boyfriend said she was fat, just used to have a drink — say fresh orange juice — at dinner. Her friends were worried that she might start suffering from Anorexia Nervosa.

Conclusion.

Many children at my school do eat a lot of fat in the form of chips, crisps and pies. Some people especially girls, will eat salads and yoghurt and so on, but they are not popular.

Recommendations.

I don't think pupils will take much notice of colour-coding but it could be tried. Showing films about what eating too much fat can do to your heart might do some good, certainly for boys I think. A healthy diet at home is very important too. If you have been used to eating a balanced diet at home, you're more likely to choose sensible food at school so parents should be educated about food too.

Jo Ann Meiling.

To what extent does the conclusion follow from the findings?

What recommendations does Jo Ann make and which does she think is of most importance?

NOTE

If, in your examination, you are expected to produce a report in essay form, you should omit the sub-headings.

5. The Speech

Occasionally, candidates are invited to write their answer to a question in the form of a speech. To do this effectively involves the following considerations:

(i) *Audience awareness*—because a speaker or a writer who communicates successfully is one who is aware of his audience. Although in an examination your real audience is the examiner, your speech must be directed at the audience specified or implied by the question. Once you have identified your audience, begin with an appropriate form of address and bear them in mind throughout your speech.

(ii) If the question requires you to put forward your viewpoint on a controversial issue, you will probably find the *language of rhetoric* helpful. Whilst logic and sound reasoning are of prime importance in a speech of this sort as much as in an essay, you may also like to make judicious use of a variety of devices:

Figurative, persuasive or emotive language
Parallels, examples or instances
Rhetorical questions
Humour, satire or irony
Exaggeration or repetition.

The trick is to use some of these sparingly, so that they will pack a greater punch.

(iii) A *well-organised, convincing argument which builds up to a climax* is crucial if the reader is to take away a favourable impression from your speech. If, as you write, you can imagine yourself actually delivering the speech, it will help you to achieve the right tone and make what you have to say sound more natural.

(iv) You may be asked to write a speech which is intended *to inform rather than to persuade*. Here, it is important that you *organise* your material well and avoid letting it degenerate into a list. Varying your sentence structure will help prevent your speech being boring. In addition, you may care to add a dash of humour and a sprinkling of colourful illustrations to ginger up what you have to say.

Sample SPEECH

You are asked to give a talk about your school to the top class of a local primary school. Many of these children will shortly be entering your school as first formers. Using **some** *of the information suggested in the following categories, write your speech.*

What you have to say should be informative. It may be lighthearted, but it should not be boring. You may add information of your own.

(a) NUMBER IN SCHOOL

Pupils
Number of teaching and ancillary staff
Type of school, age range of pupils, number of forms

(b) FACILITIES OF SCHOOL BUILDING

Date opened
Science laboratories
Art and Craft area
Library
Music and Drama Studios
Modern Languages area
Other Subject areas
Assembly hall
Gymnasium
Outdoor Sports areas
Cafeteria

(c) ORGANISATION

Faculties
Timetable
System of banding or streaming
Opportunities for extra tuition
Pastoral care system
Reports; parents' evenings; careers advice
Discipline

(d) ACTIVITIES

School trips; field courses etc.
Games matches and other sporting events
Music and drama
Clubs
Parents' Association

(e) ACHIEVEMENTS

Examination results
Games results
Contributions to the local community

Hello boys and girls. I am pleased to be here in front of you all today to tell you about my school, "Broughton High".

The school has 900 pupils and about 50 teachers. We also have some staff who do not teach; these include dinner ladies, caretakers and the cooks who make our dinners. There are children aged from just one year older than yourselves, right up to boys and girls of 16 years, and although it is much bigger than your school, you will find it extremely warm and friendly. The school is only seven years old and contains a library with a large selection of books to please you all.

We have five science laboratorys, fully equipped for all you budding scientists. The school has marvellous art and craft facilities and it would be hard to find any other school with such a high standard of sporting opportunities. Any of you wanting to play any instrument of your choice can freely do so with full teaching and important of all, encouragement. We have a cafeteria which has a wide selection of food, and with prices that are reasonable.

There are eight lessons in one day of 35 minutes each. We have a 20 minute break in the morning and one hour for dinner. At lunchtime you can attend one of the various clubs which run, or simply play in the wide area of land set aside for this purpose. Reports are given about twice a year, telling your parents about your progress. These are followed by deadly parents nights where your parents find out the real truth about you!

The average punishment at school is a lunchtime detention when you are kept inside for about half an hour to do work.

If you are the sporting type, then you will be pleased to hear of the many sporting teams for both boys and girls. Everybody is given a chance, even if they are not too good, and you know what they say, "Practice makes perfect", so if you're not all that good have a go, you'll surprise yourself in the end. These are teams such as netball, football, hockey, badminton and rugby. You are able to take drama up until the third year and there is an excellent drama room allowing all your fantasies to come to life. School discos are often arranged and we have a mini snack bar selling sweets, drinks and chocolates. These are run by the parents association

James keeps the members of his audience in mind during this speech. How many references to them can you find in the first three paragraphs for instance?

What effect does James want to have on his audience when he uses the word 'deadly'?

Can you select some points which James has made to create a lively effect?

who also arrange many other activities such as jumble sales for charity, fairs and fetes to help both the school and those in need.

The school has a superb examination passing record. All pupils are given an excellent education and really, at the end of the day, it is totally up to you as to whether you want to revise for, and therefore, pass your exams.

I hope that I have given you a reasonable idea of what goes on at Broughton High School and I also hope that you will enjoy to the full your stay with us.

James Askam

Is it possible to give a title to each paragraph in this speech?

6. The Review

When you are asked to give a review of a book, television programme or film, the choice of subject matter is almost always left to you. It is important to:

(i) *make a good choice*. Whether the question directs you to select a subject to suit a particular audience, or permits you to choose one which has general appeal, it must be a subject with which you are thoroughly familiar. Begin by giving the title of your subject and other relevant information such as its author or director.

(ii) give *a brief account of its contents*. Try to convey the atmosphere or mood of your subject by the way you write about it; thus if your subject is a comedy programme you may like to include some examples of the humour it features. Be selective about what you include; it is not usually necessary to mention every twist and turn of the plot. Make your subject interesting by picking out vivid details which exemplify it. After your summary

(iii) *give your opinion* of the quality of the book (or programme or film) by considering such aspects as setting, plot, characterisation and style. Where appropriate, you may assess more technical aspects such as skilful camera work or striking illustrations. Beware of skimping this evaluative part of your review, for not only does it show the examiner just how much thought you have given to your subject matter, it also distinguishes your work from everyone else's. Anyone can write a summary, but good candidates can employ their critical faculty wisely too.

Example

Which book, from amongst those you have read, would you choose as a birthday gift for one of your friends? Write a review of the book and explain as fully as possible why you would select it. (This is only an extract from the answer.)

Having previously purchased a copy of "The Secret Diary of Adrian Mole aged 13¾" by Sue Townsend, I decided that it would make an excellent present for a friend of mine, whose birthday was in the near future. I found the book tremendously funny and was confident my friend would find it equally amusing.

As the title of the book suggests, the most prominent character is Adrian Mole himself. Adrian is a born worrier and it seems that he carries the problems of the world on his shoulders. One of his greatest worries is his complexion, never a day seems to pass without reference to "The spot on my chin..." Throughout the book comments are frequently made on the behaviour of his parents, Mr and Mrs Mole and their not too successful marriage. These family problems obviously affect Adrian and

This piece of work contains very few errors. Can you see any of them?

Kym tells us a great deal about Adrian and his friends. Do you think she could have made her paragraphing a little more effective and, if so, how?

he is deeply worried about the way of life he finds himself leading. Despite the traumas Adrian is continually faced with, life is not all full of misery and depression. His girlfriend, Pandora, often referred to by her nickname Box, is a great companion for him and has the courage and determination to bring him out of his brooding moods. Adrian is not a boy of great popularity and excluding Pandora, his only friends are Nigel and Bert. Nigel, his supposedly best friend, is so spoilt he usually makes Adrian jealous and angry because his parents cannot afford the luxuries Nigel's can. His other friend, Bert, is an eighty-nine year old man who he regularly looks after cleaning his house and running errands for him. Adrian tends to have rather a high opinion of himself, believing he is an intellectual, a cut above everyone else. A good deal of his spare time is spent writing poetry, which he believes is a great talent of his and he often posts them to the BBC hoping that they will eventually get published.

All these disasters and seemingly dreadful situations, such as having a faceful of spots and your girlfriend two-timing you, are just a selection of misfortunes that many teenagers will find incredibly familiar and true to life. Being able to relate to the crises, which confront Adrian Mole so often, I found reading this book extremely hilarious and so accurately realistic in the descriptions of family life. Kym Wareing

Kym has an impressive vocabulary. Select and consider some examples.

This is an extract from Kym's review. She went on to explain why she felt her friend would enjoy this book.

7. The Short Story

A short story may be written in response to a variety of stimulus material. You may be given a one or two word title, such as 'Hunted!' or 'The Win', leaving you plenty of freedom as long as you remain *relevant*. Alternatively, you may have a photograph or a cartoon to set you thinking. Avoid describing only what is in the picture. Analyse it, think of ideas associated with it and give your story *structure*.

You have, at the most, *ONE* hour and about 500 words, which is not much time or space in which to produce a good story, so do try to remember the following points:

(i) *A powerful opening.* Sometimes the question supplies the opening sentence but, if not, begin with an *exciting* one and a *good first paragraph*, where the action will encourage the reader to go on. Study the openings of the stories in this book and see what you can learn from them.

(ii) *Limit plot and style* to what you can handle in an hour. Do not change the scene too often or introduce too many characters.

(iii) Successful stories can often be produced from common happenings or *ordinary experiences, told from a new and individual angle.*

(iv) *Economy in the telling* is important. This does not simply mean brevity, which can reduce a short story to little more than an anecdote.

Nonetheless, descriptions should be kept short, characters revealed through what they do and say, setting and atmosphere created through a few significant details.

> *WARNING*: Do not use dialogue unless it really advances the action and only do so at all if your punctuation is completely reliable.

(v) *The ending* may be a decisive conclusion, an unexpected turn of events or an open one which leaves the reader guessing. Whichever it is, it should give a satisfying, positive impression to the examiner, and not trail off feebly.

Example

Read on, to see how one of our students coped with a short story which began as follows:

'As the train pulled into the station, I felt exhilarated. My holiday was about to begin. Nothing would stop me from having the time of my life. I got off the train, loaded my luggage onto a trolley and made my way to the barrier, where the ticket collector held out his hand for my ticket. I looked amongst my belongings for my black holdall. But where was it—and where were my tickets, my money and my passport?'

How many references to the narrator's feelings can you find on this page?

Desperately, I turned, I retraced the several yards back to the track, my eyes searching frantically. The plane was leaving at 10.52; that left me with just under two hours. Panic rose inside me, as again I foraged among the other luggage and scanned the floor, picking up every little detail.

That bag held every important thing needed for my holiday, the main item being a passport. Without train tickets I could not even leave the station platform, they had also been lost. I felt scared. The station was a hive of business and a cacophany of sounds reached my ears; yet amongst all these people, I felt alone. Pulling myself together I saw a porter.

"Excuse me! Can you help? I've lost my bag."

"Lost property is that way miss", was the useful reply.

I made my way in the direction he had indicated and saw a small hot, hagged looking old woman sat inside.

"Have you had a black holdall handed in by any chance?"

"Sorry, no bags been handed in today lovey".

Again my hopes fell. The chance of my holiday in Spain seemed to be decreasing with every heart beat! What now? I couldn't even pay for a train home since all my money was in the holdall.

I stood there feeling and looking lost. Apart from asking every single person I saw if they had seen a black holdall, there was nothing else I could do.

But then I noticed a train drawing in on a line which led to storage sheds. Something in me sensed that it was the one I had travelled on. Feeling elated I began to run, pushing my luggage trolley in front of me, and getting it stuck in cracks on the tiled floor.

"Stop, stop!" I yelled.

Pick out the first reference to the bag and consider the effect of putting it where it is.

Look at the nine pieces of direct speech in this story. How are they linked to the narrative? [Are there lots of 'he said's and 'she said's? If not, why not]

The train halted and I received several black looks from onlookers, as I clambered on. In desparation, I flung open door after door now, quite exhausted. For the life of me I could not find the carriage I had been in. I wasn't even sure if it was the right train.

"Excuse me, miss, is this what your looking for?"

I turned to face a young girl of about ten. In her hand was a black holdall. Mine!

"Oh! Thankyou!" was my exclamation, as I took it from her. I searched it and took five pounds out of the wallet, giving it to the girl.

"What's this for?" she enquired.

"For saving my holiday!" I smiled.

Catherine Lloyd

Collect some action verbs and consider their effects.

How does Catherine maintain the suspense until the end of the story?

8. The Description

You may be invited to describe a person, a place, a time or an event. The stimulus material may consist of a picture, a short passage or a poem. (If a poem does appear on the examination paper, remember that you must not write a poem in response to the question. You may be permitted to do so if you are taking the course work option of your syllabus, but your teacher must advise you about this.) On the other hand, there may not be any stimulus material apart from the question itself.

(i) It is best to *begin by identifying the subject of the description exactly*. 'Write a description of a winter scene, stressing how different it is from other seasons' is *NOT* the same as 'Write a description of winter'. If a scene is specific, it is essential to *visualize a particular scene* and to describe that, without being tempted to stray into generalisations about winter which do not relate to the scene. Similarly, if you are asked to describe a place, a person or an event, look closely at the limitations placed upon you. The question will almost certainly ask for a description of a *specific* kind of place, person or event.

(ii) *Approaching your subject-matter systematically* should result in a full description. Describing a person, for example, will probably involve supplying some information about the person's appearance, personality, behaviour, idiosyncrasies, relationships with others, interests, preferences, pet hates and so on. Describing an event invariably involves giving an account of it as well as painting a verbal picture of it. If your subject is a scene or a season or a particular time of day, you may find the five senses method (that is, describing what can be seen, heard, touched, tasted or smelled) will give your work shape. Alternatively, the question method may be suitable; answering each of the questions, where? when? what? who? how? why? in turn, should produce sufficient organised material.

(iii) A description is the perfect vehicle for *well-observed details and for figures of speech* such as similes and metaphors. Don't be self-indulgent, however. Such figurative language creates more impact if it is used economically.

> A word of warning is necessary here. If you are asked for a description, do *NOT* tell a story.

Example

Describe the scene in a town centre on a cold winter's morning. (This is only an extract from the answer.)

What contrasts do you notice between different people's reactions to the weather?

A cold and frosty morning in the town centre prevokes nervous feelings amongst the elderly and crisp excitement amongst youngsters. Pensioners eager to return to their warm dwellings tread carefully along the icy streets, laiden with their early morning provisions. Rosy-nosed children slither over frozen puddles under the watchful eye of a caring parent. Fashion-worthy teenagers don the latest trends in sophisticated hats, multi-coloured scarves and fingerless gloves, creating a sea of bobbing colours which gush through the town centre towards the nearest warm café. Courtly-dressed commuters dash precariously from the warmth of their Inter-city to an awaiting taxi, passing the raw-faced salesman as he sets up his "Hot Potato" stand.

Through the crisp foot steps of adventurous shoppers emerges the shrill chatterings of starlings as they perch upon the town hall and office windows in search of warmth or food. Venturing outside the security of the town's public buildings, they find the odd breadcrumb or titbit lying on the circumference of the frozen duck-pond in the centre of the park. Early morning joggers can be seen circling the pond in a mist of steamy breath and excess heat accompanied by the occasional 'quack' from the resident mallards. The surrounding trees and ground are covered with a clinging frost, sparkling like a carpet of diamonds. The air is crisp and misty as the sun fights a losing battle attempting to destroy Jack Frost's creation and restore the pond to its natural habitat, housing noisy ducks and the occasional swan. Toddlers, too young to have experienced schooling, are seen running gaily through the winter wonderland, exceeding their guardians in both enjoyment and energy! Amusing themselves by impersonating fiery dragons with the sight of their steamy breath.

Back in the town centre, the shops have come to life as the colourful lights and tempting heat invite shoppers to venture inside just for a gaze around. Hats, mittens, boots and scarves are selling as fast as the hot potatoes, combating the chilly wind blowing in from the east.

So, as you can see, on a cold, winter's morning in the heart of the town centre temperaments are as varied as the colourful fashions. Apprehension and despair on behalf of the elderly and excitement and enjoyment amongst the young.

Joanne
Parkinson

Joanne loves using the adjective-plus-noun construction. Select a few examples. Which do you think are most effective?

How is this paragraph linked with the first one?

9. The Account of a Personal Experience

There is usually at least one opportunity on the examination paper for candidates to write from personal experience. Our experiences, although they may be similar to other people's, are unique and we can often write about them very perceptively, simply because of our direct involvement. Those candidates who lack the confidence to tackle a short story or a description will probably find that they can write fluently about a personal experience. Frequently the planning of this kind of writing presents few problems, because it follows a clear-cut sequence of events.

(i) It is easiest to *choose an experience which involved few people.* Explain the background to the situation and then recount what happened.

(ii) Try to *convey as honestly as you can the attitudes and behaviour of all the people involved.* The reader can only see what you enable him to see. Think of yourself, not just as a participant in the experience, but also as a camera recording what happened in as dispassionate a way as possible. Focus on significant details of the appearance and behaviour of the others who were there. Give the reader 'close-ups' of particularly telling moments.

(iii) *Explain, too, how you felt* at different stages of the experience. Try to make the whole incident *real* again. If you can do that, you will have produced a convincing piece of writing.

> Where the wording of the question specifies a personal experience, you must write about a personal experience and *NOT* give a far-fetched, fictionalised account of some unlikely event.

Example

'As I entered the room, I was very worried. What on earth was I going to say?'

Give an account of a meeting or an interview, the prospect of which filled you with dread. Describe your feelings before, during and after the event.

Look at the first sentence in each paragraph. How does Gemma keep the account of this experience moving along?

I can hardly describe my feelings. I suppose I was excited, terrified and exhilarated, all rolled into one. For a start, I had never been without Mum or Dad for a weekend, let alone two weeks. Now, I was on my way to Germany to stay with my penfriend and I would not see my parents for fourteen days!

Sitting on the plane, I felt lonely, and upset at my departure from the family. Even the new experience of flying could not make me feel any elation.

Pick out the references Gemma makes to her feelings.

At Zürich airport Martina greeted me in a friendly way, putting me at ease for a while. We chatted about England and about what we were to do and see over the next couple of weeks. In a taxi it was half an hour to Martina's home in Germany, I hardly noticed it. When we reached her house, it occured to me that I was about to meet her family for the first time. I was suddenly frightened. My German was not particulary good, and from what I could gather, neither was their English! Home was my main aspect of thought. Why had I agreed to come?

We were standing in the hall, and Martina indicated a door. As I entered the room, I was very worried. What on earth was I going to say? Six pairs of eyes pierced into me, and I wondered what they thought. Was I dressed to their liking? Was I shaking?

Collect the questions. Why does Gemma use them?

"H, h, hello." I managed to stammer, forgetting they were foreign. I stood there, smiling, and wanting to run out.

A kindly looking woman asked a question in German. I did not understand and responded with a nod of the head, hoping it was enough. She had obviously asked if I would like a cup of tea, and now she had begun to pour me one. I did not dare say that I could not stand tea. Martina chaperoned me to a chair, where I thankfully took the weight from my feet. Still, nobody spoke and still I smiled.

Pick out a word used in an unusual way and consider its effect.

Relief fell upon me, when at last Martina began to chat, in English. At least now I could talk to her, and not appear dumb, or rude! Within half an hour I felt more at home, and even though I could not understand half of what was said I managed to make some sort of reply. Usually a "Ja" or "Nein." Even so, I was glad to retire to my room and unpack.

Looking back, I appear to have made a mess of the whole thing. However, I realise that they understood my feelings. During the whole fortnight that was the only time that I had problems and from then on I had the time of my life. They were an extremely lovely family and next year I hope to return there. Meeting a family, especially foreign, proves to be terribly nerve racking, but after the initial stages, everything turns out to be fine, well, it did in my case.

Gemma Orme

Can you divide this account up, to show how Gemma has answered the question?

David: 'I think examiners are like normal people,
but they have an advanced academic brain.'

UNDERSTANDING

In this chapter we shall consider the kinds of questions which are intended to test your understanding of what you read. There is always at least one comprehension passage in the GCSE English examination, but there may be two or three passages. The examination in comprehension may consist *entirely* of an objective multiple choice test or it may *include* this type of test along with others. The subject-matter of the passage or passages may be either literary or non-literary in character. Depending on your syllabus, you may be expected to provide one of your answers in the form of a set of notes, or you may be asked to discuss aspects of one or two advertisements. All these features of comprehension we shall deal with under the following headings:

1. The Objective Multiple Choice Test

2. The Comprehension

3. Making Notes in Comprehensions

4. Advertisements in Comprehensions

1. The Objective Multiple Choice Test

If the syllabus you are following contains an objective multiple choice test, it may consist of questions—twenty-five to forty in number—on one or two passages. For each question, the candidate is offered four or five alternative answers from which he must select the correct one.

(i) As in all comprehension exercises, it is vital that you *begin by reading through the passage (or passages) several times*. Then *read each question carefully*. It may appear to you initially that two or three of the alternative answers are correct, but remember that you are looking for the *most appropriate* answer. How do you find it?

(ii) The trick is to *locate in the passage exactly the material you need to work out the answer*. More often than not you will be given a line reference in the question. Re-read the whole of the sentence which contains that line. Think about what it means. Then, try out each of the alternative answers in that context. Sometimes, it is not enough to re-read the whole sentence. You may have to re-read a paragraph, or even the last

and first sentences of adjacent paragraphs, to ensure you have the whole context you need to work out the most appropriate answer. If you take pains to do this re-reading thoroughly, you are *much* more likely to select the correct alternative.

(iii) You will probably find that one or two of the suggested answers are obviously inappropriate and that two of the remainder both seem appropriate. At this point, *read the question again* very carefully. Work out what it means by putting it into your own words. Then see which of the two possible answers *corresponds in every respect* to the question.

(iv) If you are still uncertain about the correct answer, *make a guess*. You may choose the wrong answer rather than the right one, but any answer is far better than none.

(v) The questions tend to be a combination of the following types, but not all are necessarily found in the same test.
You may be faced with:

—questions which ask for the *meaning* of a particular word or phrase *in its context*.
For example: 'Which one of the following is closest in meaning to—as used in the passage?'

—questions which ask you to find a *reason* to account for some occurrence or idea.
An example of this kind is: 'Dr Mark Smith was appointed because—'

—questions about the *literal and metaphorical use of language* such as:
'Which one of the following words is used literally rather than metaphorically?'
You may also be asked more specifically about types of figurative language such as the simile, the pun and the uses of hyperbole and personification.

—questions about the particular *use of certain punctuation marks* and *of italics*.
You may encounter questions like: 'The semicolon after 'varieties' (line—) could most suitably be replaced by—'

—questions which ask you *to sum up* the contents of a paragraph or *to identify its main idea*.

Examples are: 'Which one of the following best summarises the content of the paragraph?'; 'The first paragraph conveys the idea that—'

—questions which require the candidate *to infer the right answer*, that is, *to read between the lines* of the passage. This kind may read: 'The inference in line— is that the richer customers—'

—*'eliminator'* questions in which all the alternatives are correct except one; the wrong answer is the right one, if you see what we mean!

Their format is: 'All the following are true EXCEPT—'

—*'negative'* questions, which are usually along the lines of: 'Mass media' (line—) does NOT include—', are similar to 'eliminators'. Here again, the wrong answer is the right one.

—*'combined'* questions, which demand more thought than most of the other types, because two or three of the possible statements *together* make up the correct answer.

(vi) *A special answer sheet*, which is marked by computer, accompanies each objective multiple choice test and the candidate uses an HB pencil to fill in the boxes, which, in his view, correspond to the correct answers. If you have never completed this kind of test before, you may find it helpful to study the instructions found on the Associated Examining Board/South-East Regional Examinations Board comprehension paper which follows. These directions will give you a good idea of the procedure which is generally adopted, though there may be minor variations in the multiple choice test you take.

ASSOCIATED EXAMINING BOARD
for the General Certificate of Education

THE SOUTH-EAST REGIONAL EXAMINATIONS BOARD
for the Certificate of Secondary Education

Joint Examination for the General Certificate of Education (Ordinary Level)
and the Certificate of Secondary Education

ENGLISH

44/1

Paper I—Comprehension

Tuesday, 5th June, 1984

Time allowed: 1 hour

40 questions. Answer all questions

IF, AFTER READING THIS PAGE, YOU DO NOT UNDERSTAND ANY POINT, ASK YOUR TEACHER.

1. Use only an HB pencil and do NOT rub out.

2. Write your name and the Subject Title in block capitals in the spaces provided on the answer sheet.

3. Make sure each line you mark on the answer sheet is black and clear.

4. In the blank boxes provided on the answer sheet write:

   (i) your Centre Number,

   (ii) your Index Number.

   Mark these Numbers in the boxes as shown in the example ─────→

Centre number	Index number
2 7 1 0 5	8 0 3

5. Read each question and the answers which follow it; then decide on the answer.

6. Each question has only ONE correct answer which will score ONE mark.

7. Begin at question 1 and work steadily through the paper.

8. On your answer sheet the black numbers refer to the questions and the pink letters to the possible answers.

9. Find on the answer sheet the number of the question you are answering.

10. Show your answer on the answer sheet by joining up the marks of the letter you have chosen with a straight line. For example, if you think the answer to question 8 is D, you should mark the answer sheet like this:

11. If you want to change an answer after you have marked the answer sheet, shade the whole of the lower part of the box you have marked and mark the letter you now think is correct. For example, if you now think the answer to question 8 is B you should mark the answer sheet like this:

8 ·A· ─B─ ·C· ▉

12. Do all rough working in this booklet.

13. If you cannot answer a question, go on to the next one.

14. When you have reached the last question, go back and attempt any questions you have left unanswered.

PASSAGE A

Read the following passage and answer questions 1–20 on the test paper. The questions refer only to the words, meanings or ideas of the writer as expressed in the passage given.

Late one October afternoon in the year 1924 a shabby young man gazed with fixed intensity through the window of a third class compartment in the almost empty train labouring up the Penowell Valley from Swansea. All that day Manson had travelled from the North, changing at Carlisle and Shrewsbury, yet the final stage of his tedious journey to South Wales found him strung to a still greater excitement by the prospects of his post, the first of his medical career, in this strange, disfigured country.   5

Outside, a heavy rainstorm came blinding down between the mountains which rose on either side of the single railway track. The mountain tops were hidden in a grey waste of sky but their sides, scarred by ore workings, fell black and desolate, blemished by great heaps of slag on which a few dirty sheep wandered in vain hope of pasture. No bush, no blade of vegetation was visible. The trees, seen in the fading light, were gaunt and stunted spectres. At a bend of the line the red glare of a foundry flashed into sight, illuminating a score of workmen stripped to the waist, their   10
torsos straining, arms upraised to strike. Though the scene was swiftly lost behind the huddled top gear of a mine, a sense of power persisted, tense and vivid. Manson drew a long breath. He felt an answering surge of effort, a sudden overwhelming exhilaration springing from the hope and promise of the future.

Darkness had fallen, emphasising the strangeness and remoteness of the scene when, half an hour later, the engine panted into Drineffy. He had arrived at last. Gripping his bag, Manson leaped from the train and walked quickly   15
down the platform, searching eagerly for some sign of welcome. At the station exit, beneath a wind-blown lamp, a yellow-faced old man in a square hat and a long nightshirt of a mackintosh stood waiting. He inspected Manson with a jaundiced eye and his voice, when it came, was reluctant.

"You Doctor Page's new assistant?"

"That's right. Manson. Andrew Manson is the name!"   20

"Huh! Mine's Thomas, Old Thomas they mostly call me, dang 'em. I got the gig here. Set in—unless you'd rayther swim."

Manson slung his bag up and climbed into the battered gig behind a tall angular black horse. Thomas followed, took the reins and addressed the horse.

"Hue-up, Taffy!" he said.   25

They drove off through the town which, though Andrew tried keenly to discern its outline, presented in the lashing rain no more than a blurred huddle of low grey houses ranged beneath the high and ever present mountains. For several minutes the old groom did not speak but continued to dart pessimistic glances at Andrew from beneath the dripping brim of his hat. He bore no resemblance to the smart coachman of a successful doctor but was, on the contrary, wizened and slovenly, and all the time he gave off a peculiar yet powerful odour of the stable. At last he   30
said:

"Only jest got your parchment, eh?"

Andrew nodded.

"I knowed it." Old Thomas spat. His triumph made him more gravely communicative. "Last assistant went ten days ago. Mostly they don't stop."   35

"Why?" Despite his nervousness, Andrew smiled.

"Work's too hard for one thing, I reckon."

"And for another?"

"You'll find out!" A moment later, as a guide might indicate a fine cathedral, Thomas lifted his whip and pointed to the end of a row of houses where, from a small lighted doorway a cloud of steam was emerging. "See that. That   40
there's the missus and my little homestead. She takes in washin' like." A secret amusement twitched his long upper lip. "Reckon you might want to know, shortly."

Here the main street ended and, turning up a short uneven side-road, they boggled across a piece of pit ground, and entered the narrow drive of a house which stood amongst the adjacent rows behind a stunted ash tree. On the gate was the name Bryngower.   45

(From '*The Citadel*' by A. J. Cronin)

Detach the sheet from the back of this booklet and use it in answering the following questions

Questions 1–20 refer to Passage A (Page 7)

1. 'Labouring' (line 2) suggests that the train was
   - A carrying very few passengers
   - B heavily laden
   - C travelling uphill
   - D mostly carrying working men

2. The journey (line 3) is best described as
   - A wearisome
   - B roundabout
   - C exciting
   - D eventful

3. The phrase 'the prospects of his post' (line 4) suggests that Manson
   - A was enjoying the journey
   - B had received an important letter
   - C would be involved in mining
   - D was taking up an appointment

4. The country is described as 'disfigured' (line 5) largely because of the
   - A black mountains
   - B industrial waste
   - C bad weather
   - D mine shafts

5. In the first paragraph, Manson is described as all of the following EXCEPT
   - A bored
   - B youthful
   - C poorly dressed
   - D very excited

6. The mountain sides (line 7) were all the following EXCEPT
   - A dark in colour
   - B hidden by clouds
   - C bare of vegetation
   - D dotted with slag heaps

7. 'Blemished' (line 8) is nearest in meaning to
   - A covered
   - B decorated
   - C dotted
   - D spoiled

8. The sheep (line 8) were all of the following EXCEPT
   - A hoping to find food
   - B grazing on the mountain
   - C unlikely to find any food
   - D roaming on the slag heaps

9. The trees (line 9) are compared with

    A   sights

    B   ghosts

    C   giants

    D   watchers

10. Manson was looking to the future (line 13) with

    A   great apprehension

    B   much energy

    C   much uncertainty

    D   great expectation

11. 'Emphasising' (line 14) is nearest in meaning to

    A   contrasting

    B   disguising

    C   exaggerating

    D   stressing

12. The scene (line 14) is described as strange and remote mainly because

    A   it was unlike anything Manson had seen before

    B   Manson was not used to railway stations

    C   Manson had seen it only in daylight before

    D   it was a long way from Manson's home

13. The mackintosh (line 17) is identified with a nightshirt probably because

    A   Thomas was wearing it at night

    B   it was of similar material

    C   it was long and shapeless

    D   Thomas looked ready for bed

14. The manner in which he inspected Manson (line 17) suggests that Thomas

    A   was prejudiced against Manson

    B   had only one good eye

    C   had a serious illness

    D   was jealous of Manson

15. Thomas's greeting to Manson (line 19) is best described as

    A   belligerent

    B   cordial

    C   grudging

    D   welcoming

16. 'Discern' (line 26) is nearest in meaning to

    A   discover

    B   distinguish

    C   observe

    D   recognise

17. Andrew's nod (line 33) confirms that he had

    A   only recently qualified

    B   recently had a drink

    C   just obtained a post

    D   only just arrived

Turn over
44/1

18. Thomas's triumph (line 34) was because he

    A   persuaded Manson to answer his question

    B   had spat accurately

    C   had guessed correctly

    D   knew Manson would not stay long

19. We are told in the passage that Drineffy has all the following EXCEPT

    A   grey houses

    B   a railway station

    C   a cathedral

    D   nearby mountains

20. Which one of the following is used figuratively rather than literally ?

    A   'the engine panted into Drineffy' (lines 14–15)

    B   'beneath a wind-blown lamp' (line 16)

    C   'a peculiar yet powerful odour of the stable' (line 30)

    D   'from a small lighted doorway' (line 40)

Vanessa: 'An examiner must have a high I.Q. and wear glasses. I also imagine him to be overweight.'

2. The Comprehension

The examination paper in comprehension may consist of:

one passage,

OR two passages, each with a set of questions,

OR one passage with questions plus several shorter passages, linked by a common theme, which share a set of questions.

The subject-matter of each passage may be:

literary (for example, a short story or an extract from a novel, biography or autobiography)

OR non-literary (for example, a newspaper article or a verbatim news report from television or radio).

Where there is a great volume of reading matter on the paper, sufficient time is allowed for you to read it all thoroughly. Depending on the syllabus you take, you may be permitted to use a dictionary in the examination.

(i) *Begin by reading the passage carefully, at least twice.* (If you are allowed a dictionary, use it to check on the meaning of any word you don't understand. Make sure you find the meaning of the word in its *context* or else you may get a misleading impression.)

(ii) Next, *read through all the questions.* Obviously you cannot receive credit for using the same material in more than one answer, so it is vital to locate the *relevant* material in the passage. The question may direct you to look at certain lines or paragraphs; the answer you need will be contained in them or in lines near them. Do not be tempted to stray to other sections of the passage, or you could be using material you need for another answer.

If the question does not specify in which lines or paragraphs the answer is to be found, remember that most of the questions in a comprehension are arranged in a logical sequence to correspond with the subject-matter of the passage. The early questions are often the most factual and the final questions usually invite a broader view of the passage or even ask for some kind of 'directed' writing. Where a question demands material which occurs at various points throughout the passage, it is especially important not to include any material you have used in a previous answer.

(iii) *Take note of the number of marks allocated to each question.* Each mark generally represents one point that you have to make, although sometimes examiners also give marks for clarity of expression, logical sequencing or style. *Answer in full sentences* where possible and ensure that the answer is related to the question e.g. Q: What is the industry of the town?

A: The industry of the town is ...

(iv) *Let the number of available marks dictate the length of your answer.* If, for instance, there are five marks, it is foolish to answer with one brief sentence, since you are unlikely to cover five points in this way. To score all the points, it may be necessary to write five *short* sentences. In general, a full answer is preferable to a very short answer, *provided it is neither repetitive nor irrelevant.*

Sometimes one question may carry *far more* marks than any of the others. To answer such a question fully may involve writing up to a side in length, particularly if you have to write a letter or provide a set of notes. Here again, however, your main concern should not be the length of your answer but the number of points it contains.

(v) **Never leave a question unanswered or incomplete.** Try really hard to make as many points as there are marks. If you cannot find them all, make an educated guess. You may be half right and half a mark is better than none, especially in an examination!

(vi) It is preferable to **use your own words** wherever possible, even if you are not specifically asked to do so. In some examinations, marks are halved or withheld if the candidate has 'lifted' directly from the original passage. Apart from running the risk of losing marks, it is best not to lift straight from the passage because the process of translating the original into your own words is the real heart of comprehension. If you *can* paraphrase it, you can almost certainly understand it and your answer will be all the better for your having made the effort.

(vii) Beware, however, of the question which asks you to '*quote*'. This means precisely what it says and if you misguidedly use your own words in this kind of answer, you will not receive any marks for it. A pity—but that's life!

(viii) Where you are asked to give the meanings of a series of words or phrases **as they are used in the passage**, remember:

(a) to give *EXACTLY* the number you are supposed to. Giving more than you need is a waste of time and giving fewer is a waste of marks.

(b) to test out each explanation by substituting it in the passage for the original word or phrase. (If it doesn't fit, change it so that it does.)

(c) to check (especially in the case of single words) that your explanation is precisely the same part of speech.

(ix) The kinds of questions you will encounter will include:

—questions which require straightforward *information* from the passage.

—questions which ask you to *reorganise information* in some way, by expressing facts, ideas or arguments in your own words.

—questions which ask you to *infer*, in other words, to read between the lines of the passage.

—questions in which you are required to *compare* or *contrast* two sections of a passage, or two passages, or part of a passage with your own experience. In the process of comparison, you may be asked to *evaluate* the reading material.

—questions about the writer's use of language, the style and the structure of the piece.

—questions which invite you to demonstrate *empathy* with the reading matter by your ability to put yourself in the position of one of the characters in a story and to appreciate his/her situation.

—questions about the writer's *intention*, whether it is to inform, to persuade, to entertain and so on.

3. Making Notes in Comprehensions

Sometimes you may be asked to give the answer to a question as a summary in the form of notes. Often such answers are worth a considerable number of marks so it is as well to spend some time doing the notes as efficiently as you can. To answer the question properly, you have to ANALYSE the material, SELECT the writer's main ideas and important details and ARRANGE them according to the writer's argument in a logical way.

(i) Find in the passage the section which you have to summarise in note form and read it several times, picking out the *theme sentences* or *main ideas* in each paragraph. You may find it helpful to underline these twice in pencil. These will become the basis of the *main headings* in the notes.

(ii) Next, look for *ideas of lesser importance*, which will be the basis of the *sub-headings* in the notes. You could, perhaps, underline these once, in pencil.

(iii) Then pick out *important details*, particularly those which are *examples* or evidence to support each main idea. You may like to put brackets round these.

(iv) Now you should *paraphrase* (that is, put into your own words) and *abbreviate* the writer's main and less important ideas, as far as possible. This is important because notes are, after all, another means of testing that you have understood the passage.

(v) *Set out your notes* so that the logic of the writer's line of argument is clear. Use plenty of space, leaving some lines empty if you like. You may, of course, use standard abbreviations. In note form below, is a summary of how to set out notes.

Your own finished notes should look something like this:

SETTING OUT NOTES

A. <u>TO SET OUT HEADINGS</u>

1. *Main Headings*
   (a) represent main ideas
   (b) use capital letters and/or underline them
   (c) start at margin

2. *Sub-headings*
   (a) represent ideas of lesser importance
   (b) use lower case letters and underline them
   (c) indent a little from margin
   N.B. Indent e.g.s still further.

B. <u>TO SHOW RELATIONSHIPS</u>

1. *Use Different Headings*
see above

2. *Itemize*

(a) for main ideas use:
  (i) Large Roman Numerals (I, II, III, etc.)
OR (ii) Capital Letters (A, B, C, etc.)

(b) for ideas of lesser importance use:
  (i) Arabic Numerals (1, 2, 3, etc.)
OR (ii) Lower Case Letters (a, b, c, etc.)

(c) for examples/evidence use:
  Small Roman Numerals (i, ii, iii, etc.)

Taking Notes in Aural Comprehension

Since your ability to produce good answers in an aural comprehension depends not just on the reliability of your memory but also upon the accuracy of the notes you make, practising *active* note-taking is advisable. You may find it useful to bear in mind that:

(i) *abbreviations*—standard ones and those you make up for your own use—are invaluable. Some people abbreviate in notes by *writing down the first (and perhaps the second) syllable of a word and its last letter only*, e.g.

lib^y = library
sec^y = secondary
prop^l = proposal
beg^g = beginning.

Others abbreviate by *omitting vowels and vowel sounds*, e.g.

bk = book
shld = should
cld = could
wk = week.

A few words can be replaced by *single letters or signs*, e.g.

u = you
r = are
c = see
= = means/is the same as
? = question/ask/doubtful.

Whilst the meaning of some of these abbreviations may be ambiguous out of context, *in context* their meaning is usually obvious. What counts is that *you* remember the meaning of your abbreviations for the duration of the test.

(ii) It is better to *leave out structural words*, such as pronouns, auxiliary verbs, prepositions and conjunctions. Note down *key facts* and *striking details* only, that is, nouns, adjectives, main verbs and adverbs.

N.B. Notes such as these which contain abbreviated forms which are personal to you and which are not generally understood would, obviously, NOT be suitable for inclusion in notes prepared for anybody else.

4. Advertisements in Comprehensions

Occasionally an advertisement is included in a comprehension exercise and you are expected to answer one or two questions about it. Often these questions concern the effectiveness of the advertisement and the method by which it makes its appeal. Sometimes the questions ask you about a link between the advertisement and the subject-matter of the passage which usually precedes it. Within the limited space available to us here, it is impossible for us to examine the vast subject of advertising in depth. What we can try to do, however, is bring to your attention a number of its significant aspects so that you will have some idea of what to look for in an advertisement in the examination.

(i) Advertisements frequently have *two meanings*, an ostensible one— one that lies *on* the surface—and a latent one—one that lies *beneath* the surface. If you are to spot these meanings, you need to look closely at the words and the *picture(s)*.

Choose 3 or 4 advertisements from newspapers and magazines and think about, and comment on, some of the following aspects:

WORDS

Name of product/service; what does that suggest?
  e.g. Silver Spoon (sugar), Vogue (bathroom fittings)
Quantity of words and size of lettering in relation to size of picture(s);
Type of lettering, if unusual;
To what extent do words *inform* and to what extent do they *persuade*?
Use of *words with consumer-appeal*, e.g. natural, free, fresh, bright, healthy.

PICTURE(S)

Use of *black/white/* or *colour*—especially, gold, white and other strong colours;

Is *product/service* featured *in picture* or is it *absent*?

Focus of attention in picture; any pattern apparent in content of picture?

Relationship between picture(s) and words: if no words, what message does picture convey? If neither words nor product/service featured in advertisement, how does picture sell product/service?

If person featured in picture, what kind of person is he/she? Age? Degree of attractiveness? Social status? State of health? Financial status?

(ii) Advertisements make their appeal in a variety of ways.

Here are some of them:

A correlation may be indicated between a particular product and some other desirable item so that the product becomes desirable too. There may be an *emotional correlation*—a connection between the product and our feelings.

Some products are promoted on the basis of their *exchange value*; if we buy Product X, we buy something else we desire too.

Other products are intended to appeal to *a particular group of people*, perhaps on the basis of the product's exclusiveness or snob value. Alternatively, some advertisements appeal to us as *unique individuals*, playing on our urge to discover our ideal self.

Nature is utilised in many advertisements. It may be copied or transformed but it is usually improved upon by the product! Sometimes we are shown how we can obtain 'natural goodness' from a particular product whilst other products are depicted as battling against or withstanding the onslaught of nature.

Science, with its connotations of prestige, detachment and independence, comes to the adman's aid too. Some advertisements supply us with figures and so-called scientific facts—and spurious objectivity. Ask yourself when you are looking at this kind of advertisement whether or not scientific knowledge is really being offered or whether it is merely being referred to.

Then there is *magic*, with which the adman can weave spells, effect transformations and turn a little into a lot.

He can make use of *time* too—time past, in myths, in history and in personal memories, and time future, when, after we have bought Product X, all our dreams will come true!

Mark: 'An examiner is a very serious, clever and studious person who sets devious questions. He looks like a typical old English master from Eton or Harrow.'

SPOKEN ENGLISH

Many candidates feel apprehensive about undertaking the oral assignments which are a compulsory part of GCSE English examinations. Often this is because they are self-conscious about giving a talk or a reading in front of their classmates. This is hardly surprising when teachers do most of the talking that goes on in classrooms whilst pupils, mostly, listen!

The great majority of candidates are capable of achieving a satisfactory standard in spoken English, so there is no reason why, with sound preparation and sufficient practice, *YOU* should not. It is worth remembering that the oral element of the examination can carry a considerable percentage of the total marks (depending on the syllabus you take) so it is only common sense to invest enough time and effort in it.

Each candidate is assessed in at least two ways in spoken English but often he is required to undertake a wide variety of oral assignments, individually and in collaboration with others, during his course. Most, if not all, of these assessments are carried out by the candidate's teacher during routine English lessons. There is time, then, for each candidate to gain in confidence and to improve his performances in spoken English.

Listed below are some of the oral assignments you may be asked to do during the year leading up to the examination.

Individual Assignments	Group Assignments
Talk	Discussion
Conversation (candidate plus examiner)	Conversation (more than one candidate)
Reading	Debate
Aural comprehension	Problem-solving exercise
Story-telling	Mock trial
Monologue	Duologue
Mock news reading/ reporting	Mock press conference
Commentary	Panel games (e.g. Any Questions)
Presenting a taped magazine programme	Taped magazine programme
	Interview
	Improvised drama
	Scripted drama

In this chapter we shall concentrate on the five principal ways of assessing spoken English and suggest how you may improve your performance.

Let us look in turn at 1. the talk, 2. the conversation, 3. the reading, 4. aural comprehension and 5. group discussion.

1. Giving a Talk

Preparation: *Select a subject which really interests YOU.* If you can be enthusiastic about it, your audience will probably respond with enthusiasm too. Your subject should have some depth to it, as your talk has to last about five minutes (check your syllabus for the precise time limit) and you have to be able to answer questions on it.

One of the following suggestions may appeal to you:

—a travel talk

—a biography of a well-known person

—a review of a good book or film

—a demonstration of how to do something

—a talk about your hobby or interest

—a talk in which you put forward your point of view on a controversial issue

—a talk in which you supply information about a subject not especially well-known to the audience

—an account of a personal experience

Research your subject well—not just from one source, but from several. A talk on a holiday you enjoyed can be enhanced by some background information on the place and by the reactions to the holiday of others who went. You may accumulate too much information, but knowing more than you hope to say will boost your confidence and provide you with ample material with which to answer searching questions. If you discover at this stage that there is a lack of suitable material on your chosen subject, abandon it and choose another. You cannot score highly on shallow, limited subject matter.

Collect together any materials which may supplement your talk visually—photographs, posters, diagrams, drawings, objects or models. These should be big enough for people at the back of the room to see and, of course, they should be relevant and supportive to what you have to say.

Planning: Just as a piece of continuous writing should be *well-organised*, so too should a talk. If your research has produced a lot more material than you can cover in about five minutes, concentrate on one aspect of the subject. A thorough treatment of a narrower subject is better than a very superficial treatment of a wider issue.

You will probably find it useful to break down your material into *four, five or six key elements, stages or ideas* and to arrange these so that your talk will follow a logical progression. You may work out in detail what you intend to say about each of the key items but *DO NOT WRITE OUT YOUR TALK IN FULL*. This could be disastrous as you might be tempted to read it to your audience and doing this would lose marks. To help you remember the points you are most likely to forget, you could jot down on several postcards (one card per key item) *BRIEF NOTES*—single words, phrases, statistics.

Visual aids can give you confidence, provided they are good ones which serve to illuminate your talk, rather than to distract your audience's attention. So plan the use of your visual aids in conjunction with what you intend to say.

Some items may be mounted on large sheets of sugar paper or thin card. These can then be stuck to a wall at the front of the classroom with Blu-Tack or Buddies. You could make large maps or diagrams on sugar paper too, or on the blackboard. Any objects you intend to show are best arranged in the order in which you will use them. If you are giving a demonstration, collect everything you will need, and assess whether it would be useful to prepare a few items in advance to illustrate various stages of the process you are describing.

On the whole, it is best to be economical in your selection of visual aids. Too many can be confusing both for you and your audience, and in fact they are not essential. One of our students gave an imaginative and original talk on 'Hands' with no other aids than her own hands. Because her subject-matter was thought-provoking, full and well-organised, and because she talked about it so fluently and humorously, she scored a very creditable grade.

It is not a good idea to use live animals, which can be unpredictable and distracting, nor to use anything valuable or fragile. It would be a pity if some prized family heirloom were lost, damaged or stolen whilst in your possession.

Practice: This is advisable. Practise your talk at home in front of a mirror or your family to iron out any unforeseen problems which might put you off, were they to occur in class. Beware of too much practice and avoid learning your talk off by heart. It could well be penalised if it gives the impression of sounding like an essay. Try to anticipate the questions you may be asked and work out roughly what you might reply.

Performance: Keep calm (easy to say, we know, but do try!), take a few deep breaths, arrange your visual aids and any notes you may have on the table in front of you, and then, when you feel quite ready, begin to speak. Face your audience squarely, because good eye contact with them is very important. (If you find this too unnerving, find someone or something at the back of the room you can look at without flinching.)

Obviously you should try to begin with an interesting opening sentence and not the usual, boring 'My talk is on . . .'. Make sure that the subject and scope of your talk are clear at the outset.

Your use of language, the volume and clarity of your voice, and your posture are very important in creating a good impression, so try not to be sloppy about any of them. If you have prepared your talk well, without actually learning it off by heart, what you say will retain the necessary degree of spontaneity. Anecdotes, especially personal ones, which are relevant to your subject-matter, can help liven up your talk and give it individuality—essential if someone else has chosen to speak on the same or a similar topic. Leave something unsaid, so that members of the audience are able to ask you questions. Remember to use your visual aids to demonstrate what you are saying, but it is wise not to pass items round the class whilst you are talking. It is better to do this during question time.

Your teacher will tell you how long your talk should be. Do try to stick to this limit. Talks which are substantially shorter or longer than they should be can incur penalties because they are badly organised.

At the end of your talk, finish off strongly by drawing what you have said to some kind of conclusion or by referring to some point you made at the outset, showing you have made a connection between that and the end. You may even like to finish with some completely new or surprising information or idea, to leave your audience with something to think about.

When your talk is over, give all your attention to the questions and answer them as fully as you can. If someone thoughtlessly asks you a closed question—that is, one to which a one or two word answer seems the only possible response—try to expand your answer by supplying additional information or ideas. Remember, you can often earn extra marks on your ability to answer questions. That could mean the difference between scoring an average grade or a good one.

What is the examiner looking for in a good talk?

> A well-prepared, well-organised talk, which demonstrates a knowledge of the chosen subject and which is delivered with confidence, good eye contact and appropriate vocabulary will earn a good mark. In addition, the talk must be clearly audible and may make use of well-chosen visual aids. The talk should be interesting to the audience and the questions which follow it should be answered fully.

2. The Conversation Test

Conversation tests vary, so we shall look at two main types. For the first kind of conversation test, candidates submit a topic of their choice to the examiner, or they may opt to give an introductory talk, although no credit is given for the

Shaun: 'The examiner is the sort of person who would enjoy sitting at home on examination day thinking of all the panic he is inflicting on young people everywhere.'

talk itself. For the second kind of test, candidates first have to read a short passage, chosen from a selection provided by the examination board. In addition, they must furnish the examiner with some information about their hobbies, interests, ambitions and so on. The conversation will include some discussion of the reading passage, as well as of the personal information supplied by the candidates. Generally, this kind of test is taped, but try not to let that put you off!

Type one

Preparation: If you opt to give an introductory talk, you will probably find it helpful to read through the suggestions we make in **1. Giving a Talk.** Your teacher will advise you about the precise requirements of the syllabus you are following. If you decide to submit a topic without first giving a talk, choose a subject with which not only you, but the examiner, will be familiar. The choice of an obscure, technical or specialised subject can be a disadvantage, if your listener, through lack of knowledge, is unable to put pertinent questions to you.

Practice: Once you have chosen your topic, it is up to you to ensure you know enough about it to be able to anticipate the questions which may be put to you. It may be wise to talk over with someone the main elements of the topic before the test, so that you are alerted to areas in which you have not clearly thought out your ideas.

Type two

Preparation: You may be invited to make a choice from the selection of reading passages available, but you may also be guided in your choice by your teacher. Your reading will probably be graded. For further advice on how to accomplish a competent performance, read **3. Giving a Reading** later in this chapter.

Most of the test will concern the personal information you have submitted in advance, so anything which is a little out of the ordinary could make the conversation more interesting and stimulating for both of you. It is important to note that, in this kind of test, you are not encouraged to prepare lengthy statements about your subject-matter in advance.

Practice: The examiner will probably want to broaden the scope of the conversation, perhaps by putting forward a controversial viewpoint related to one of your interests or ambitions. He may also want to generalise from the particular information you have supplied. Here he will be looking to see if you can follow his lead by thinking about the subject-matter in a more general, less personal way. Perhaps someone you know will help you to work out what you might say by asking you some general questions. The best kind of practice, of course, is taking every opportunity to talk, in a relaxed way, to adults—in and out of school—so that you will feel more at ease in the test with the examiner.

Types one and two

Performance: For successful communication to take place, you must be positive non-verbally as well as verbally. In other words, the way you sit should indicate your interest in what is taking place during the conversation. You should maintain good eye contact with your partner and your face should show interest too.

Listen carefully to the points raised by your partner. Try to give full, relevant replies but if you do not altogether understand what he is getting at, ask him to explain. Carry the conversation forward by introducing new material wherever it seems appropriate. This means you should volunteer information or ideas, so that your partner is provided with fresh insight into your interest in the chosen topic.

The language you use is important. You do not have to pretend to be someone you are not, but you do have to share responsibility for the conversation by expressing yourself clearly and correctly.

What is the examiner looking for in a good conversation test candidate?

Type one: A good candidate is one whose subject is well-chosen and substantial, who has the ability to carry the conversation forward and to establish a good relationship with the listener. In addition, he should be able to express himself properly and to speak clearly.

Type two: A good candidate is one who can respond with well-structured answers which vary in length and complexity, whose vocabulary is wide, appropriate and imaginative and who, in discussion, can express himself logically and objectively, supplying, where necessary, suitable examples in support of his views. Such a candidate will speak clearly and, by virtue of his lively contribution to the conversation, will be capable of holding the interviewer's attention completely.

---

3. Giving a Reading

Under (A) below we deal with the type of reading test which precedes a conversation test. (B) covers the kind of reading test in which the candidate chooses his own passage.

(A)

Preparation: Usually a selection of short passages (containing about 250 words) is available, from which you must choose one, a few minutes before you are to read it to the examiner. Your teacher may guide your choice, basing it upon his knowledge of your interests and reading preferences. The subject-matter may be factual, possibly adapted from a newspaper article, or it may be an extract taken from a novel or short story.

Practice: Scan the passage quickly to acquaint yourself with the subject-matter. It may have a distinctive mood, which you must identify and try to convey. It may contain dialogue which must be read convincingly. It will almost certainly contain sentences which vary in length and complexity, and these should guide the pace of your reading and influence your intonation. To give a successful reading of the passage, you have to show that you *understand* it.

Next, read the passage *SLOWLY*, paying special attention to commas, full-stops and any dialogue it contains. Look for any difficult or unusual vocabulary and say these words quietly, but aloud, to yourself to check your pronunciation. If time permits, read the whole passage through again, quietly, but aloud, to yourself to see if you are pacing it properly and achieving the right degree of emphasis, wherever it is appropriate.

Performance: For advice on this, read what we suggest under this heading for (B).

(B)

Preparation: In this kind of test, the choice of reading is left entirely to you. *The importance of a good choice cannot be overestimated*, since you must select a long extract, generally of about 500 words (check your syllabus), to read to an audience of your classmates, as well as to the examiner. If you have read widely during your course, this should present few problems for you. You must, of course, have read the book from which your extract comes, because you will have to answer a few questions on it.

Planning: Look through your book for a passage of the right length which is 'a whole', that is, an incident or a description which out of context still retains sufficient significance to arouse the interest of an audience who will probably not have read the book. Select a strong passage, which, because of its humour, tension, drama, conflict, or novelty might well make the audience want to read the book. It must also be as self-explanatory as possible because, although you will be able to set the scene in your introduction, this must be done briefly. A lengthy introduction, by its very nature, undermines your choice at the outset.

Look, too, for a passage in which there is some variety of sentence structure. Without such variety, your reading is likely to be rather boring for your audience and this will prevent you from demonstrating your versatility. If you can, pick a piece in which there is some dialogue—but not too much. Reading dialogue successfully involves skill in characterisation on your part—a tricky feat but one which will be rewarded with a good grade if you can pull it off.

Analyse the passage carefully. Since it is likely to be in a book of your own, you can annotate it with symbols to represent pauses, variations in volume, pitch and pace and to indicate words which require special emphasis.

Finally, work out a brief introduction in which you mention the title and author of the book and set the scene.

Practice: This is essential. Practise your passage by reading it *ALOUD* as many times as you can; in this instance, practice *can* make perfect! If you can find someone to listen to you and make helpful comments, so much the better; otherwise you might tape yourself reading and then try to analyse how you might improve. Do not be afraid of the sound of your own voice. The more you become familiar with your passage and the sound of yourself reading it, the more you will gain in confidence. If there is any dialogue, have the courage to characterise the speakers by altering the tone, accent and pitch of your voice.

Performance: Whichever type of reading test you do, you will need to perform it in much the same way. Breathe in deeply a few times to calm your nerves and to give you a good air supply with which to start. Whether you are to sit or stand during the reading, make yourself comfortable before you begin. Hold the book up to chest height and yet at a convenient distance from the body. Your face should not be obscured from the view of the audience, nor should you look down at your knees or feet as you read. Do not start to read until you feel composed.

If an introduction is permitted, deliver it clearly and confidently. (Ideally you should try to maintain some eye contact with your audience throughout your reading, and this is frequently most effective when you want to emphasize a particular point.)

Announce the title, pause and begin to read. Try to speak clearly, evenly and at a steady pace from the start. Pause slightly at commas and a little longer at full-stops. You will undoubtedly have to pause too during longer sentences which do not contain commas. Divide these up into phrases and clauses and read them so as to illuminate their meaning.

Use stress moderately and wisely. Treat dialogue as if it were part of a playscript and try to characterise the speakers. Strive to maintain the same volume and pitch with which you began, varying them only when the sense dictates. This is especially important as you approach the end of the passage. After all, the examiner awards you a grade after the *last* paragraph you read and not the first.

If you should stumble over a word, or get the pace or intonation of a particular sentence wrong, try not to let it worry you and put you off. Even radio and television news readers make mistakes like these. Only re-read that particular section if it is vital to the sense—otherwise ignore your mistake.

When you have finished reading, pause and prepare yourself to answer the questions fully and relevantly. Remember that, as with the talk, you can usually increase your grade if you answer well.

What is the examiner looking for in a good reading?

A good reading is one in which the passage has been chosen carefully and usually combines narrative and dialogue, where the candidate speaks clearly and confidently and where, by suitable changes in his pace, pitch, tone and use of emphasis, the spirit of the writer's words is conveyed. Depending on the syllabus, an introduction may be required and good eye contact may be expected.

4. The Aural Comprehension

Preparation: An aural comprehension tests your capacity both to listen and to understand. Since neither you nor your teacher will determine the content of the test, the preparations you can make must necessarily be of a limited kind. Your teacher will probably borrow, from the examination board, recordings of sample aural comprehension tests and no doubt provide opportunities for you to learn at first hand exactly what they are like.

YOU, however, can ensure that you can take good notes, quickly and methodically (see Chapter Two of this book for advice on making notes) and that you are not tired or distracted by other considerations at the time of the test itself. The ability to concentrate is of crucial importance. You have to be able to listen and to write simultaneously without using shorthand.

Practice: Aural comprehensions can consist of accounts of events, from which you have to select the significant facts or details, upon which to base a summary. Alternatively, they can consist of a duologue or other dramatisation about which you have to answer questions. Why not listen to news bulletins on radio or television and see if you can jot down details of the major items? You can easily check whether you got them right or not from a later bulletin. It will also help if you are accustomed to *listening* to plays and stories on radio, rather than simply watching them on television.

Performance: Depending upon the syllabus, the tape or record containing the passage or duologue may be played once or twice. Candidates may be allowed to read through the questions either immediately before or during one of the readings. Read the questions carefully so that you know what information you are listening for. Some of the questions may ask for only one fact or detail, whilst others may require you to organise material in much the same way as you would in a conventional comprehension. Bear in mind, too, that some of the information may be implied rather than stated directly. For instance, you may have to calculate someone's age or state someone's occupation, using fairly obvious clues given at various stages in the comprehension. Sometimes the material you need to answer an early question may occur towards the end of the recording.

Obviously the secret of success in this type of test lies in your ability to make good notes, as well as in your capacity to memorise whatever you can. To be really useful to you, your notes should be selective and relevant.

The recording will last only a few minutes. When it is over, jot down in note form any potentially relevant information you can. Then look at the questions again. In your answers, keep to the point. Depending upon the syllabus you take, you may be required to give an answer in your own words; usually this comes in a question about the meaning of a word used in the recording. More often, however, the actual vocabulary used in the test passage is acceptable.

Use the writing time (generally thirty minutes) to answer every question; a guess is better than a blank space.

What is the examiner looking for in a good aural comprehension answer paper?

> A good candidate is one who has the ability to see the point of each question and to stick to it, to produce precise, clearly expressed answers, to include relevant details *or* to be selective, as required.

5. Taking Part in a Discussion

At least one 16 + syllabus stipulates that candidates should be assessed not only as individuals but also as participants in a group oral assignment. Frequently this assignment takes the form of a discussion. So that each member of the group has a fair chance of producing a competent performance, we suggest the following procedure:

Preparation: Team up with two or three other candidates, one of whom is a chairperson who, on this occasion, is not assessed. You will need to select a topic—perhaps a contentious subject, since a successful discussion often stems from a conflict of opinion, or you might select an open-ended subject which can be explored or expanded by everyone in the group. A discussion of what makes a good parent (or a dutiful child!) is an example of this kind of subject.

Planning: Once again, research into your subject is vital. Many candidates participate in discussions with pre-conceived ideas which are not based on a sound knowledge of the facts. When their views are challenged, they are at a loss as to how to provide a convincing reply. It therefore makes sense to find out all you can about the topic well before the discussion.

You can research your subject in a number of ways. The library is an excellent place to start. Apart from the wide range of reference books available to you, official statistics in census returns or in *Social Trends* (H.M.S.O.), can be useful too. For up-to-date information on current controversial issues, you could refer to *Keesing's Contemporary Archives* and the *British Humanities Index*. Both are up-dated regularly. The former contains summaries of significant world events, whilst the latter is a record of articles written in leading newspapers and magazines on a very wide variety of topics.

By looking up your subject in the Index, you will find a list of the articles written on it and the newspapers and magazines in which they are to be found. These will almost certainly be stocked by your nearest large library, where you can either read the article you need or have it photocopied.

Perhaps the subject your group has chosen concerns a local issue. In this case you might find it helpful to canvass the opinions of as many people as you can through a short questionnaire. This is likely to produce a lot of points you can use in the discussion.

Many pressure groups, concerned with all kinds of issues at both local and national level, are willing to provide you with information about their ideas if you write to them and ask for it.

Just one word of caution, however: do make sure that you understand the *significance* of any information you intend to introduce.

You may be designated chairperson on one occasion. This involves researching the topic the rest of the group will discuss and working out some open-ended questions you can put to them, should their ideas run out. Since you will probably not be marked, you could, perhaps, write your questions down. (If you can demonstrate that you are a good chairperson, impartial, fair, well-informed and able to ask stimulating questions, your teacher will no doubt bear your performance in mind when he awards you an overall mark for your oral work throughout the course.)

Practice: Going over, with the help of a friend or relative, the points you hope to make in the discussion could clarify your thoughts and improve your powers of expression. Others will undoubtedly have formed their opinions and will be eager to express them—obviously you do not want to be lost for words or only able to intervene briefly with a question or a comment.

Performance: The chairperson will probably start the ball rolling by inviting each member of the group to make an opening statement. After that, it is up to you to concentrate on the direction the discussion takes and to contribute relevantly whenever the opportunity arises. The discussion could, and probably will, take an unexpected turn. Think hard about what the others are saying, so that you can respond appropriately. Indeed, you should try to expand the subject and introduce new ideas if the others seem to be going round in circles.

A discussion is a co-operative venture. Ideally, no one member of the group should dominate and no one should be prevented from having his say. If you find that, because you are well-prepared, you have most to contribute, do ask others how they feel about the ideas you have put forward. Then listen patiently and carefully until you are able to add something further. Neither ramble, nor be unnecessarily repetitive, and certainly do not be tempted to be abusive. Your aim, remember, is to put your viewpoint in a clear, intelligent, logical and courteous way.

What is the examiner looking for in a good discussion candidate?

> To score a good grade, you must understand the subject, be able to comment or argue relevantly, lead the discussion (perhaps even changing its direction) *and* listen as others take the lead. You should demonstrate that you can think clearly and logically and express yourself in a mature, courteous manner.

Paul: 'An examiner is a man with a tired look. He has small, red eyes, which are heavy from continuous reading. He sits in a smoke-filled room.'

PART B
PRACTICE PAPERS

Before you attempt any of these exercises, your teacher will tell you how much time you will need to spend on each question and whether you may use a dictionary.

INSTRUCTIONS VARY SLIGHTLY FROM SYLLABUS TO SYLLABUS.

Each of these eight PRACTICE PAPERS, or UNITS is divided into two parts:

EXPRESSION AND UNDERSTANDING.

Generally speaking you should allow no more than *ONE* hour on each question, including reading time.

Under examination conditions, you would only be expected to answer

ONE question from Section A and

ONE question from Section B of the EXPRESSION PAPER.

On the UNDERSTANDING PAPER you would be expected to answer *BOTH* sections.

Paper 1 Expression

Section A

A1 A Woman's Place is in the Home

A2 Working on the Oil Rigs

A3 The Willows

Section B

Essays

Paper 2 Understanding

Comprehension A:

Ha'Penny by Alan Paton

Comprehension B:

Fee Fi Fo Fum (Blood Donors)

Paper 1, Section A

A1. **A Woman's Place Is In The Home**

Many people feel that the woman's place is in the home. Here are the views of a variety of people on this subject. What are your views?

*You should refer to **some** of these opinions but you do not need to use them **all**.*

An Employer

'I'd offer a job to a man before a woman any day. Married women have their homes and children to worry about, so how could they concentrate on the job?'

Mr Brown

'I'm the breadwinner here! I don't want my wife going out to work. Besides, it's not a man's place to clean and cook.'

Mrs Brown

'How women can find the time to go out to work is beyond my understanding. There's so much to do at home, such as cleaning, washing and ironing, not to mention looking after children. Anyway, I think it's selfish of women to go out to work when there's so much unemployment about and men with families are out of work.'

Mr Green

'I certainly don't mind helping in the house whilst my wife goes out to work. There are no bills to worry about, we eat very well and, best of all, we have marvellous holidays abroad. I think I'm lucky!'

Mrs Green

'With all my labour-saving gadgets, I don't think I could find enough to do at home all day now that the children are at school. I enjoy my work and I know that this makes me a better wife and mother at home. Besides, I studied for years to obtain my professional qualifications, so it seems a waste not to put them to good use.'

Childminder

'Thank goodness some mothers do want to go out to work. It provides me with an income looking after their babies. You see, I've three children of my own and I can't find work to fit in with school holidays. Anyway, I like looking after children.'

Mrs White

'My husband doesn't earn enough to keep us. We have two children, so I have to go out to work. I wish I could afford to stay at home.'

A2. Working On The Rigs

*Five men who work on offshore oil rigs were interviewed about their jobs. The following are extracts from what they said. Read them carefully and then write an **article** on the attractions and the drawbacks of working on an off-shore rig, and on the kind of person one has to be to cope with the life. Conclude your article by giving your own views of such work, stating whether or not you would enjoy it, and the reasons for your decision.*

John

'I used to be a labourer on building sites. When the weather was bad, I'd be laid off and I didn't get paid. That's not much good for a married man. On the rigs I'm a roustabout— loading and unloading supplies and doing general labouring.

We work in all weather, even in gales. It doesn't bother me because I'm earning good money and it's regular. The accommodation's quite comfortable and the food's good.

I don't think about the dangers much. Being a coal miner is dangerous, isn't it? When you're working twelve hour shifts for fourteen days at a stretch, you just look forward to your pay cheque and to your fortnight's leave every month. Yet when people ask me what I do, I'm proud to tell them I work on the rigs.'

Tom

'It's a tough life, especially if you're a roughneck like me. My job entails labouring for the driller on the rig floor. It's dirty and noisy and sometimes I wonder why I'm out here in the middle of the North Sea, especially when a gale's blowing and we have to change drill bits . . . because the drilling never stops.

Sometimes one of the roughnecks is injured and has to be taken off the rig by helicopter, so why do I work out here? Why did men go out to the Klondike?'

George

'Diving brings me in one of the best salaries on the rig, far more than I earned in the Royal Navy. It's a challenging job—terrifying and exciting at the same time. You have to have steady nerves and be really physically fit. You feel special because very few people can do the sort of diving we do. You're in demand all over the world, so there's plenty of variety.

I couldn't stand a routine job—catching a bus every day, being in the same place year in year out.'

Pete

'Being on a rig means being part of a small, isolated community where everyone is interdependent. So you have to be able to get on with everyone. Some people might think it's like being in prison—confined to a metal platform about as big as a football ground for two weeks at a time with seventy or so other men. You can't stroll down to the pub or take your girlfriend out. But you have plenty of free time off the rig.

I enjoy my job. I'm one of the cooks and between us we're serving a full range of meals twenty-four hours a day. Our food wouldn't disgrace a first class restaurant. The menu's international because there are men from all over the world on board.'

Dave

'I was a radio officer in the Merchant Navy and was often away from home for long periods. The offer of a job on the rigs, working two weeks on and two weeks off, was very appealing.

I look after all the communications between the rig and the shore. I keep in touch with the helicopters bringing out urgent supplies or new personnel on crew change days. . .I work between twelve and fifteen hours a day and am always on call in case of emergencies. We have weekly fire drills—we never know whether it's going to be the real thing.

The main nuisance on board is the continuous high noise level from machinery drilling but another is the weather. During the winter we get bad weather for long periods, which is rather demoralising but the job has to go on. And most rigs are 'dry'—there's no drinking.

There are some compensations. As part of my job, I show newly released films three or four times a week; we have video cassettes and large screen TV; we get the daily papers and mail most days.'

A3. The Willows

Study:
  (i) The plan of 'The Willows'.
  (ii) Photograph showing the chapel and one of the Victorian houses.
  (iii) The information.
  (iv) The three proposals.

Then, after careful consideration, decide which ONE of the three proposals you would choose, explain why, and also very carefully explain why you would reject the other two proposals.

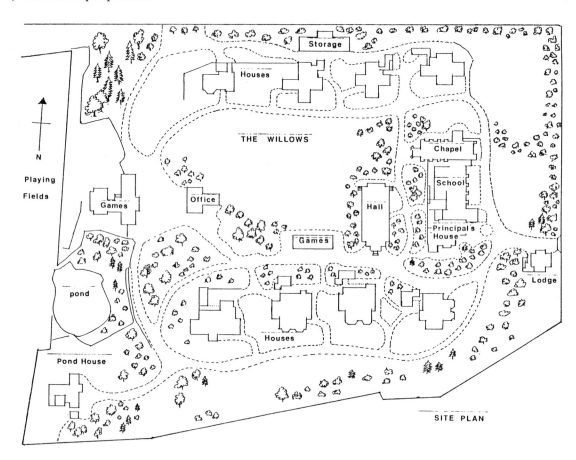

SITE PLAN

(iii) From a Trust Fund, 'The Willows' was built in 1888 as an orphanage and a school. Alongside several larger, red brick Victorian buildings, such as the school, the Chapel and Baylton Hall, nine houses were built for a hundred children. Ten years ago there were still a hundred children living there. They went to the school where they were joined by local school children. Since the majority of children in the care of the local authority are now fostered, instead of being brought up in orphanages like 'The Willows', there are no longer any children resident there and the school has functioned as an ordinary, local primary school.

This year, the local children who attended 'The Willows' have been transferred to a purpose built junior school some distance away and the Trust is left with the problem of how to make the best use of the site.

The future of this thirteen acre site is still being considered.

(iv) Here are three of the proposals:

(a) The buildings should be demolished and the site should be sold for a new housing development, in order to make money to finance other major projects in the area, undertaken by the Trust.

(b) The buildings should be adapted for use as sheltered accommodation for socially deprived people, such as the physically or mentally handicapped.

(c) The Victorian buildings and extensive grounds should have a preservation order put on them. The grounds and buildings should then be opened to the public, with facilities for exhibitions and cultural events.

Paper 1, Section B

Write about two sides on ONE of the following. Remember your aim should be to produce an imaginative and lively piece of writing.

B1. You have won a prize in a newspaper competition and it is to be presented to you by a famous celebrity. Describe the presentation.

B2. My mother.

B3. Vanished!

B4. Think of a time when a misunderstanding raised a barrier between you and someone you know. Recount what happened and how you sorted it out.

B5. You have been given ten minutes of radio time on the National No-Smoking Day to give your views on why people should give up smoking. Prepare your script. Remember you need to be very convincing if you hope to make your point.

A NATIONAL no-smoking day aimed at getting one smoker in 20 to give up the habit for good, has been set yet again.

This tenth attempt to persuade Britain's smokers to drop the habit for a day will be more widespread than any of its predecessors.

Organisers are negotiating for poster space in post offices, railway stations, and offices, as well as in the surgeries of all GPs.

A smoker's guide with tips on giving up cigarettes will be published, and dial-a-tip phone lines will be open.

B6. Imagine you have the opportunity to join a circus to learn a dangerous act. Write about your experiences.

B7. Fog.

'Over the oily swell it heaved, it rolled,
Like some foul creature, filmy, nebulous.
It pushed out streaming tentacles, took clammy hold,
Swaddled the spars, wrapped us in damp and cold,
Blotted the sun, crept round and over us.'
CROSBIE GARSTIN (1887-1930)

Describe an experience which you have had as a result of fog or mist.

B8. Baby Sitting.

B9. 'The first of April, some do say,
Is set apart for All Fool's Day,
But why the people call it so
Nor I, nor they themselves do know.'

Describe the events of a memorable April Fool's Day, or St Valentine's Day. The events may be a true account of what happened to you, or they may be imaginary.

B10. Study the photograph and write about it in any way you like.

Paper 2, Comprehension A

Read the short story below and then answer the questions which follow:

Alan Paton

Alan Paton was Principal of a large boys' reformatory in Johannesburg, and it is clearly from this experience that 'Ha'penny' is told.

Ha'penny from 'Debbie go Home' (Jonathan Cape).

1. Of the six hundred boys at the reformatory, about one hundred were from ten to fourteen years of age. My Department had from time to time expressed the intention of taking them away, and of establishing a special institution for them, more like an industrial school than a reformatory. This would have
5. been a good thing, for their offences were very trivial, and they would have been better by themselves. Had such a school been established, I should have liked to be Principal of it myself, for it would have been an easier job; small boys turn instinctively towards affection, and one controls them by it, naturally and easily.
10. Some of them, if I came near them, either on parade or in school or at football, would observe me watchfully, not directly or fully, but obliquely and secretly; sometimes I would surprise them at it, and make some small sign of recognition, which would satisfy them so that they would cease to observe me, and would give their full attention to the event of the moment. But I knew
15. that my authority was thus confirmed and strengthened.

The secret relations with them were a source of continuous pleasure to me. Had they been my own children I would no doubt have given a greater expression to it. But often I would move through the silent and orderly parade, and stand by one of them. He would look straight in front of him
20. with a little frown of concentration that expressed both childish awareness and manly indifference to my nearness. Sometimes I would tweak his ear, and he would give me a brief smile of acknowledgement, or frown with still greater concentration. It was natural, I suppose, to confine these outward expressions to the very smallest, but they were taken as symbolic, and some older boys
25. would observe them and take themselves to be included. It was a relief, when the reformatory was passing through times of turbulence and trouble, and when there was danger of estrangement between authority and boys, to make those simple and natural gestures, which were reassurances to both me and them that nothing important had changed.
30. On Sunday afternoons when I was on duty I would take my car to the reformatory and watch the free boys being signed out at the gate. This simple operation was watched by many boys not free, who would tell each other, 'In so many weeks I'll be signed out myself.' Among the watchers were always some of the small boys, and these I would take by turns in the car. We would
35. go out to the Potchefstroom Road with its ceaseless stream of traffic, and to the Baragwanath cross-roads, and come back by the Van Wyksrus road to the reformatory. I would talk to them about their families, their parents, their sisters and brothers, and I would pretend to know nothing of Durban, Port Elizabeth, Potchefstroom, and Clocolan, and ask them if these places were
40. bigger than Johannesburg.

One of the small boys was Ha'penny, and he was about twelve years old. He came from Bloemfontein and was the biggest talker of them all. His mother worked in a white person's house, and he had two brothers and two sisters. His brothers were Richard and Dickie, and his sisters Anna and Mina.

45. 'Richard and Dickie?' I asked.

'Yes, meneer.'

'In English,' I said, 'Richard and Dickie are the same name.'

When we returned to the reformatory, I sent for Ha'penny's papers; there it was plainly set down, Ha'penny was a waif, with no relatives at all. He had

50. been taken in from one home to another, but he was naughty and uncontrollable, and eventually had taken to pilfering at the market.

I then sent for the Letter Book, and found that Ha'penny wrote regularly, or rather that others wrote for him till he could write himself, to Mrs. Betty Maarman, of 48 Vlak Street, Bloemfontein. But Mrs. Maarman had never

55. once replied to him. When questioned, he had said, perhaps she is sick. I sat down and wrote at once to the Social Welfare Officer at Bloemfontein, asking him to investigate.

The next time I had Ha'penny out in the car I questioned him again about his family. And he told me the same as before, his mother, Richard and

60. Dickie, Anna and Mina. But he softened the 'D' of Dickie, so that it sounded now like Tickie.

'I thought you said Dickie,' I said.

'I said Tickie,' he said.

He watched me with concealed apprehension, and I came to the conclusion

65. that this waif of Bloemfontein was a clever boy, who had told me a story that was all imagination, and had changed one single letter of it to make it safe from any question. And I thought I understood it all too, that he was ashamed of being without a family and had invented them all, so that no one might discover that he was fatherless and motherless and that no one in the world

70. cared whether he was alive or dead. This gave me a strong feeling for him, and I went out of my way to manifest towards him that fatherly care that the State, though not in those words, had enjoined upon me by giving me this job.

Then the letter came from the Social Welfare Officer in Bloemfontein, saying that Mrs. Betty Maarman of 48 Vlak Street was a real person, and that

75. she had four children, Richard and Dickie, Anna and Mina, but that Ha'penny was no child of hers, and she knew him only as a derelict of the streets. She had never answered his letters, because he wrote to her as 'Mother', and she was no mother of his, nor did she wish to play any such role. She was a decent woman, a faithful member of the church, and she had

80. no thought of corrupting her family by letting them have anything to do with such a child.

But Ha'penny seemed to me anything but the usual delinquent; his desire to have a family was so strong, and his reformatory record was so blameless, and his anxiety to please and obey so great, that I began to feel a great duty

85. towards him. Therefore I asked him about his 'mother'.

He could not speak enough of her, nor with too high praise. She was loving, honest, and strict. Her home was clean. She had affection for all her children. It was clear that the homeless child, even as he had attached himself to me, would have attached himself to her; he had observed her even as he had

90. observed me, but did not know the secret of how to open her heart, so that she would take him in, and save him from the lonely life that he led.

'Why did you steal when you had such a mother?' I asked.

He could not answer that; not all his brains nor his courage could find an answer to such a question, for he knew that with such a mother he would not

95. have stolen at all.

'The boy's name is Dickie,' I said, 'not Tickie.'

And then he knew the deception was revealed. Another boy might have said, 'I told you it was Dickie,' but he was too intelligent for that; he knew that if I had established that the boy's name was Dickie, I must have estab-
100. lished other things too. I was shocked by the immediate and visible effect of my action. His whole brave assurance died within him, and he stood there exposed, not as a liar, but as a homeless child who had surrounded himself with mother, brothers, and sisters, who did not exist. I had shattered the very foundations of his pride, and his sense of human significance.

105. He fell sick at once, and the doctor said it was tuberculosis. I wrote at once to Mrs. Maarman, telling her the whole story, of how this small boy had observed her, and had decided that she was the person he desired for his mother. But she wrote back saying that she could take no responsibility for him. For one thing, Ha'penny was a Mosuto, and she was a coloured woman;
110. for another, she had never had a child in trouble, and how could she take such a boy?

Tuberculosis is a strange thing; sometimes it manifests itself suddenly in the most unlikely host, and swiftly sweeps to the end. Ha'penny withdrew himself from the world, from all Principals and mothers, and the doctor said there
115. was little hope. In desperation I sent money for Mrs. Maarman to come.

She was a decent, homely woman, and, seeing that the situation was serious, she, without fuss or embarrassment, adopted Ha'penny for her own. The whole reformatory accepted her as his mother. She sat the whole day with him, and talked to him of Richard and Dickie, Anna and Mina, and how they
120. were all waiting for him to come home. She poured out her affection on him, and had no fear of his sickness, nor did she allow it to prevent her from satisfying his hunger to be owned. She talked to him of what they would do when he came back, and how he would go to the school, and what they would buy for Guy Fawkes night.

125. He in his turn gave his whole attention to her, and when I visited him he was grateful, but I had passed out of his world. I felt judged in that I had sensed only the existence and not the measure of his desire. I wished I had done something sooner, more wise, more prodigal.

We buried him on the reformatory farm, and Mrs. Maarman said to me,
130. 'When you put up the cross, put he was my son.'

'I'm ashamed,' she said, 'that I wouldn't take him.'

'The sickness,' I said, 'the sickness would have come.'

'No,' she said, shaking her head with certainty. 'It wouldn't have come. And if it had come at home, it would have been different.'

135. So she left for Bloemfontein, after her strange visit to a reformatory. And I was left too, with the resolve to be more prodigal in the task that the State, though not in so many words, had enjoined upon me.

Ha'penny by Alan Paton

1. Read lines 1—6 ('Of the six hundred boys ....
.... better by themselves.').

(a) What does the author, Alan Paton, say that his Department
intended to do? (2)

(b) Why would this have been a good thing? (2)

2. Between lines 16 and 29 ('The secret relations with them ....
important had changed.'), the author talks about 'The secret relations' that
he had with the younger boys.

Summarize what these secret relations were and say why they were valuable.
(6)

3. What does Alan Paton mean when he describes Ha'Penny as 'the
biggest talker of them all'? In reality, who was Ha'penny? (6)

4. From lines 58 to 72 ('The next time .... by giving me this job.')

What did Alan Paton conclude about Ha'penny and what did he
think he understood about him? (4)

5. In this story, it is not easy to decide what kind of a person Mrs. Maarman
was:

(a) How did she appear to Ha'penny? (5)

(b) What is Mrs. Maarman's view of Ha'penny, and what does Alan Paton
reveal of her attitude to him at later points in the story? (5)

6. When Ha'penny's deception was revealed, the results were such that the
author was 'shocked by the immediate and visible effect' of his action.

Describe the results. (5)

7. In this story, Alan Paton admits that he failed to recognize Ha'penny's deep
need to belong to a family. In the last paragraph he vows to behave differently
in the future. What mistakes do you think he is unlikely to make again?(5)

40 Marks

Paper 2, Comprehension B

Read the following passage and the advertisement which accompanies it, then answer the questions below.

Fee, Fi, Fo, Fum

When it came to blood, the giant in 'Jack and the Beanstalk' knew a thing or two. His nose led him to the blood of an Englishman and, in medical terms, his preference was
5. soundly based. For as far as blood donation is concerned, the blood of the English—and of every other person who lives in the British Isles—is best. You may be forgiven for thinking that this sounds like chestbeating
10. jingoism but the fact is that the blood of unpaid volunteers is superior in quality to that collected from those who are paid for it. Why, you may ask, are we buying blood? Isn't our national blood transfusion service,
15. with its village-hall methods of collection, providing enough?

The problem is that, although we in Britain are self-sufficient in blood, thanks to two million voluntary donations each
20. year from the three per cent of the population who are blood donors, we import between half and a quarter of the blood *products* we need annually. Unfortunately, on occasion, these imported blood products
25. are contaminated.

The reason that imported products carry a risk of infection is that much of the blood comes from the United States where it is bought in the main from the poor or from
30. Skid Row degenerates who have nothing else to sell. The one billion dollar-a-year U.S. blood products industry, which fulfils 75 per cent of the world's plasma needs, relies heavily on donors who, according to

35. Professor Richard Titmuss (The Gift Relationship, 1970), are described in medical journals as 'narcotic-takers, dope-addicts, liars, unemployed derelicts, prison narcotic users, bums, the faceless, the undernourished
40. and the unwashed, junkies, hustlers and ooze-for-booze donors'.

Blood donors who are drug addicts, or alcoholics, or carriers of diseases such as hepatitis and malaria are as much a danger
45. to themselves as they are to those who receive their blood. Ironically, however, the plasmaphoresis technique, upon which the U.S. blood industry is based, encourages donors to sell their blood frequently, every
50. three days if they wish. This technique, instead of removing whole blood, removes the plasma which the body can replace quickly, and returns red cells and white cells to the donor's bloodstream. From the
55. plasma, products such as Factor 8, the clotting agent, and albumin, for burns victims, are made.

Blood specialists in Britain would like to utilise plasmaphoresis much more widely.
60. To do so, teams of dedicated donors, willing to give blood at least once a month, instead of three or four times a year, must be recruited. Whilst the plan may strain the gift relationship to its limit, it must be carried
65. out if those in Britain, such as haemophiliacs, who receive blood fairly often, are not to live in fear of contaminated foreign imports.

LIKE ANY 8 YEAR OLD BOY, WAYNE MOGGERIDGE IS A LITTLE DEVIL.

One evening early last year, a couple of mates called round for Wayne.

While they were out playing, Wayne came into contact with a car – travelling in the opposite direction. Thirty feet later, he was lying in a pool of blood by the side of the road.

He was rushed to hospital where X-rays revealed that one of his kidneys had been virtually pulverised. Nearly half his liver had been destroyed. And he'd broken his leg in two places.

Wayne was also suffering from severe internal bleeding and was transferred to the Royal Manchester Children's Hospital.

To keep his blood pressure up and stop him going into shock, the anaesthetist who accompanied Wayne had to pump blood into him continually.

By the time the surgeon at the Royal Manchester got to him, blood leaking from his kidney and liver had completely distended his abdomen.

"I had only ever seen two cases like this before," said the surgeon, "and in both cases the child died."

Up until now, Wayne had received about 11 pints of blood; roughly three times the amount he normally has in his body.

The surgeon called for more.

"The amount of blood leaking into his abdomen had reached such a

LAST YEAR 40 BLOOD DONORS STOPPED HIM BECOMING A LITTLE ANGEL.

level that to open him up would have resulted in a dramatic loss in blood pressure."

During the removal of his kidney and the damaged portion of liver, Wayne was having massive blood transfusions. His body was acting as a funnel. No sooner was blood pumped into him than the same amount leaked out from his damaged organs.

Finally, at about 3 o'clock in the morning, the worst was over.

The operation wasn't. By this time, so much blood had gone in and out of his body, there were no clotting factors left.

These factors, Platelets and Factor 8, can only be obtained from plasma which can only be obtained from blood.

Wayne was given large amounts of these until his body was able to manufacture its own.

Three days later, his blood loss had dropped to a safe level and his condition was satisfactory.

In all, we gave Wayne about 30 pints of blood and blood-related substances.

Equivalent to the amount 40 blood donors had given us.

And Wayne?

Today, over a year later, only the scars remain. Wayne has bounced right back into being a normal, healthy young boy.

Quite the little devil in fact.

Questions 1 to 7 refer to the passage

1. What is the connection between blood and the giant in 'Jack and the Beanstalk'? (2)

2. Why, according to the first paragraph, is blood of British donors 'best'?

(2)

3. Look at lines 17 to 41.

(i) Why is it unnecessary for us in Britain to import blood yet necessary for us to import blood products? (2)

(ii) Why are imported blood products sometimes inferior? (1)

4. According to the third paragraph, American blood is frequently obtained from unsuitable donors. Using your own words, say what *kinds* of people these donors are. (5)

5. Look at paragraph four.

(i) What is plasmaphoresis? (2)

(ii) What are the products obtained from plasma? (2)

(iii) What are the disadvantages of plasmaphoresis as used in the United States? (2)

6. According to the last paragraph, how and why do British blood specialists intend to use plasmaphoresis? (3)

7. Explain the meaning of *TWO* of the following phrases as they are used in the passage:

chest-beating jingoism (line 9-10)
village-hall methods of collection (line 15) (6)
Skid Row degenerates (line 30)
strain the gift relationship to its limit (line 63-64)

Questions 8 to 10 refer to the advertisement on page 64

8. Look at the first three paragraphs. Explain, in your own words as far as possible, what happened to Wayne. (4)

9. Read through the remainder of the advertisement. How does it attempt to hold the reader's interest? (5)

10. The purpose of this advertisement is to encourage more people to become blood donors. By considering the advertisement as a whole, say to what extent you consider it achieves its purpose. Give your reasons. (4)

40 Marks

Paper 1 Expression

Section A

A1 Miners

A2 Cruelty to Children

A3 A Hike in the Country

Section B

Essays

Paper 2 Understanding

Comprehension A:

Berry Holly by Sid Chaplin

Comprehension B:

Hologram Holidays and Calls to the Cooker

Paper 1, Section A

A1. Miners

*Coal mining has always been hard and dangerous work. Read the following comments and then discuss the ways in which the lives of coal miners and their families have changed. Say whether or not you would enjoy such a life yourself. You should refer to **some** of the information given here but you need not refer to it all.*

Extracts from George Orwell's 'The Road to Wigan Pier' (1937)

'You get into a cage, which is a steel box about as wide as a telephone box and two or three times as long. It holds ten men but they pack it like pilchards in a tin and a tall man cannot stand upright in it. . .When you crawl out at the bottom you are perhaps four hundred yards underground'.

'Even when you watch the process of coal extraction you probably only watch it for a short time, and it is not until you begin making a few calculations that you realize what a stupendous task "fillers" are performing. . .When I am digging trenches in my garden, if I shift two tons of earth during the afternoon, I feel that I have earned my tea. But earth is tractable stuff compared with coal, and I don't have to work kneeling down, a thousand feet underground, in suffocating heat and swallowing coal dust with every breath I take; nor do I have to walk a mile bent double before I begin.'

A Retired Miner

'In the old days mining was very frightening. I went down the pit at fourteen and I hated it.

Three weeks after starting, there was a roof fall and two of the men were trapped. We'd almost freed them when there was another fall and we had to scurry away. I shall never forget the screams of those two men as they died. I wouldn't recommend coal mining to anyone.'

Working Miner

'Things have changed in mining. It's still dangerous work and it's definitely a man's job, but today the pay and conditions are better. Miners turn up in casual wear, even in suits and ties. We have changing rooms and showers, and at most pits, we are supplied with clean working clothes each week.'

Miner's Wife

'All the men in my family are in mining and I married a miner. It seemed the natural thing to do. When we got married, we didn't think of moving away; we weren't as adventurous as young people today. I never thought about the job being dangerous until Joe had an accident. Because of Joe being on shift work, I've never had a job; he needs a good meal when he's been working. In the early days, he didn't bring much money home and it was hard work washing his pit clothes. But now the pay is better, his work's not as hard and he comes home clean.'

A Deputy

'We're proud to be miners; the men are a good lot to work with. I know some can be rough but they are loyal and tough. Mining still separates the weak from the strong. Yes! Even with improved conditions.'

A2. Cruelty To Children

*Read the following article carefully and then write **a letter to the editor** saying how far you agree or disagree with the recommendation that parentcraft should be taught in schools and colleges. Suggest other ways in which the problem of child abuse might be tackled.*

Lessons needed to stop cruelty.

Recent research shows an increase in neglect of children, and in child abuse, both emotional and physical. Some of the reasons seem to be parents who are too young, marital instability, unemployment and large families.

If "Parentcraft" were added to the timetable in schools, children could learn about the stresses and problems of being a parent to counterbalance the image of parents shown on T.V. commercials.

Facts published by the N.S.P.C.C. (The National Society for the Prevention of Cruelty to Children) highlight important aspects of child abuse. There is an increase in the number of parents who themselves contact the N.S.P.C.C. after hurting their children, or feeling that they might do so.

One mother, after constantly screaming at her six-year-old son over a period of time, eventually hit him. She hit him so hard across the face that he began to bleed and needed stitches. She was so upset that she telephoned her local branch of the N.S.P.C.C. and had several months' counselling, during which it was discovered that she was trying to cope with both marital and financial problems. As a result she could not cope with her young son. He was taken into care.

Another of the stories about abused children tells of two young children being left in the house one evening. One of the children let in an N.S.P.C.C. inspector who found that his feet stuck to the carpet, which was covered with dog and cat excreta. There was dirty clothing everywhere, no food and the furniture was poor and sparse. The family had a ten year history of neglect and so the children were taken into care.

The N.S.P.C.C. claims that the four most important stress factors in child abuse are: debts, poor parental self-esteem, unemployment and marriage problems.

Practical programmes to prepare teenagers for being parents would help them to realise that being a good parent requires a wide range of skills. It is no good teaching young people the mechanics of sex in biology lessons, without also teaching them about relationships and how to cope with crying babies.

A3. A Hike in the Country

Study the map below.

You are one of a small group of people, whose ages range from 12 to 18, planning a hike from Wentworth to Upper Hoyland. You have been asked for your views on the best route to take.

*First of all, describe each of the **three possible** routes including as many details as you can. You may add any additional information you feel would be appropriate.*

*Secondly, recommend the **best** route, in your opinion, giving your reasons.*

UPPER HOYLAND

farm track

scree slopes

fishing boating swimming

cairn

pier

main road

2

3

WENTWORTH

start here

1

KEY:
1. Lakeside amble
2. Moderate hike
3. Steep climb

Paper 1, Section B

Write about two sides on ONE of the following. Remember your aim should be to produce an imaginative and lively piece of writing.

B1. The most memorable OR the most upsetting moment of my life.

B2. The Auction.

B3.

ENCHANTING...UNFORGETTABLE...
FOREST HOLIDAYS.

Watch the magic of sunset from your own cabin in the forest. A perfect end to a day exploring adventure trails and secret streams, or pony-trekking, fishing or canoeing or simply absorbing the peace of the forest.

Our fully equipped timber cabins are furnished to a high standard. All sleep 5 or 6.

Holiday houses and cottages are also available.

We can offer a comfortable base for an unforgettable holiday. Take your pick from a selection of sites throughout Scotland.

Phone for full details and FREE colour brochure 031-334 2576 (office hrs) 031-334 0066 (24 hrs).

Or for further information write to:
Forest Holidays (Dept S.C.A.)
231 Corstorphine Road
Edinburgh
EH12 7AT

Forestry Commission

No one knows forests
like the people who grow them.

You take advantage of this advertisement. Describe what it was *really* like!

B4. You offer to be a collector for a National Charity on their flag day. It is the first time you have done this. Describe your collecting adventures.

B5. Describe a visit to your capital city.

B6. It is quite common to hear people saying that they are bored. Write about a time when you fully expected to be bored but it turned out to be interesting instead.

B7. Travelling people.

B8. You are invited to join a well-known sporting personality during a day of routine training. Narrate your adventures.

B9. Write a story, real or imaginary, which finishes in this way: 'I shall always regret going back!'

B10. Study the photographs below and overleaf and write about them in any way you like.

Paper 2, Comprehension A

Read the short story below and then answer the questions which follow.

The Berry Holly by **Sid Chaplin** from 'Loves, Hopes and Fears' (Longman)

All alone in the hen-run above Nutty Hag Row the boy worked hard at plucking the chickens, which his grandfather had killed before going off to his afternoon shift in the drift mine which hummed and jangled at the end of the street.

5. The old stove was cherry red, heating the water which, poured over the chickens, made them easier to pluck. But still it was hard work, and cold, as the feathers flew. After every third chicken he allowed himself a rest, straightening his back and letting his eye rove.

First he looked over the depot where coal streamed into the big-wheeled
10. cowcarts while the shire horses stamped and blew, then along the curve of the red-roofed street to the river, very deep and black under the lea of the steep wooded hill where the old dam held it back, then widening and becoming white-flecked where the stepping-stones were that led to old Jawblades pit, so near and yet so far away.

15. There the countryside opened out and with it the sky, awesomely wide and cold with pink combs of cloud, and the sun red and very remote. In his second pause his heart gave a leap at the sight of a man crossing the river, preceded by a greyhound. The man moved hesitantly and clumsily, but the greyhound was fluid, stepping out delicately and smoothly, flowing over the stones.

20. Because of what Jawblades meant to the boy he cheated and kept constant watch on the pair as they advanced along the riverside path, the dog ranging freely ahead and sometimes streaking across the stubbled fields or sniffing in hedgerows, the man trudging with his head down, deep in thought. When he lost them he grieved. Then he forgot himself in the work.

25. Suddenly there came a scraping and he turned to find the greyhound reared high on her hind legs as if set to climb, lapping and looking through the penfold with large intelligent eyes.

And there was his father standing with his legs apart and his hands in his pockets, his jacket bulging at one side, his smile lopsided as well. "You've
30. got a shippin' order there," he remarked and came through. The greyhound whinged. "Settle!" said the man, and the dog immediately lay down on the frost-encrusted grass with her chin between her paws. The man silently took the other pail from the stove and set to, plucking two birds to the boy's one. The chickens drawn and hung in the scrubbed shed, the man lit a cigarette.
35. "Your Mam around?" he asked casually.

"She's at Auntie Polly's," said the boy. "We're goin' to gather berry holly." The man upturned a bucket and smoked broodingly. "Mind if I come with ye?" he asked at last; and the boy smiled. "Then say nowt to your Grandma," said the man, "We'll meet at the end of the street."
40. The man was waiting, not at the end of the street as promised but along the gleaming tub-track, just at the bend where the rope passed around a guide wheel. They trudged between the rails silently.

When the footpath diverged away from the black deep hole in the rockface the man took the boy's hand and helped him up the steep slope. They went
45. through the five-barred gate with ice tears hanging on the undersides of the cross-bars, past Hutchinson's farm where the cattle in the home field surged towards them, then followed the road as it wound and dropped darkly into Bellburn Wood; and only then did the man relinquish the boy's hand.

In the distance was the old air-shaft and the two cottages, in one of which
50. lived Aunt Polly. "Go on," said the man. "I'll meet you at the berry holly."

"Should Ah—should Ah tell her?" The man shrugged and turned into the wood, the greyhound ranging ahead and snuffling in the heaped leaves under the trees. When the boy arrived, dragging his mother by the hand, he had already cut several grand sprays of holly thick with scarlet berry. "Oh, you've
55. left none for us!" said the boy; and the man smiled and handed him the knife he had been using, a heavy horn-handled knife with a corkscrew, as well as the large curved shining blade.

"Ah've left you some on the bottom branches," he said.

"Golly, that's a good knife!" said the boy and started looking for sprays,
60. ducking in and out of the great umbrella-like spread of the holly bush.

"Well, and what brings you here?" he heard his mother say.

"Thought it'd be nice to get the holly berry, same as we used to." said the man, adding with a rush: "And mebbe spend Christmas together."

"You've got a hope, indeed you have," said the woman bitterly; and the
65. boy's heart gave a thump. "We're settled and comfortable—and at least we're *thought of*—not put next to a thing like that!" she concluded with a swift pure look of hate at the dog.

"You could be boss in your house," he said, and in spite of herself her eyes shone. "Ah've never had a better cavil. The money's good. Ah'll turn a fresh
70. leaf. Ah'll get rid of the dog," said the man passionately.

"Get rid of the dog," she mocked. "It'd soon find its way back—and so would the master—back to the gamblin', the boozin' an' the rest of it. And then what? We'd sharp be back on our beam ends again ..."

"Ah mean it this time, lass!" he broke in urgently. He looked at the
75. greyhound with a queer, wild kind of desperation. "Ah've run her for the last time. Ah've made a packet and squared off with the lenders. It's a clean start ..."

"It'll need some thinkin' about," she said, darkly brooding.

"It's now or never," he said, stooping to gather the berry holly. They went
80. back through the dark wood and dusk was falling as they neared Aunt Polly's. The dusk was setting in, but the berries stood out among the glossy green leaves, perfectly round and blood scarlet among the needle points.

At the air-shaft the man stopped. "Here, lad, take these," he said, handing over his burden of berry holly. "Ah'll wait here."
85. "You might as well come in and have a cup of tea," urged the woman, in a softer tone than she had hitherto used. But the man shook his head. "Ah'll be waitin' here," he told them.

As the boy followed his mother into the house he heard a sharp whistle and looked back to see the man kneeling by the old air-shaft. The light was smoke-
90. blue and all was quiet. His father was reaching into the bulky poacher's pocket of his jacket. The greyhound came running, then stopped. His father spoke caressingly and she went strangely to him, not sinuously in her own proud way but drag-legged with her ears laid back.

He heard his father murmur something, softly, as the creature came near.
95. Then he went into the bright warmth of Aunt Polly's kitchen, and marvelled at the way the streamers all gold and red stretched out from the mistletoe,

which hung like a great glowing bush upside down from the ceiling, with pears and apples of gold and silver bright upon it.

The dull clap came plain, and Aunt Polly paused with the cup at her lips. "It'll
100. be old Hutchinson and his lads after a bit of something for Christmas," said she. "Such demons with guns!"

The boy and his mother looked at each other. Then flushing and with a glance at Aunt Polly, she said: "Go and bring your father. Go, canny lad." He needed no second bidding.
105. His father was standing with his face against the air-shaft wall, and his arms hung straight down. There was no sign of the dog, but on the frost-encrusted grass little red globules shone. He stooped to touch, and his father turned. "Don't touch, lad!"

Then, wiping one hand on the wall, he said. "Ah couldn't let her die
110. hard—now could Ah?" Not understanding, the boy said yes. What filled *his* mind was that they were together again. But long afterwards it all came back—the dog swift to run, the holly berry on the ground, and a man that turned his face to the wall, and cried. Then he saw what a fortunate child he was, and what manner of father he had, and knew what the berry holly meant,
115. the berry and the thorns.

Berry Holly by **Sid Chaplin**

1. Between lines 1 and 19 ('All alone in .... flowing over the stones.'), we learn that the boy rests from his hard work on two occasions:

(a) What is he doing? (1)

(b) Using your own words as far as possible, describe what he sees each time as he rests. (3)

2. From lines 15 to 48 ('There the countryside opened out .... relinquish the boy's hand.'), what do we learn about the feelings of the father and the son for each other? (5)

3. Using evidence given in lines 62 to 87 ("'Thought it'd be nice to get the holly berry"'...................."Ah'll be waitin' here," he told them.'):

(a) explain why the boy's parents had split up.

(b) say at which point you feel that they might get back together again.(10)

4. The father had a special relationship with his greyhound. Describe this relationship by referring closely to the story and say when you first realised that he was going to shoot the dog. Why do you think he did shoot it?(10)

5. What did Aunt Polly think had happened when she'd heard the shot?(2)

6. In line 103 ("'Go and bring your father. Go, canny lad." He needed no second bidding.'), why do you think the boy's mother refers to her son as a *canny* lad? (2)

7. In the last sentence, the boy says that he 'knew what the berry holly meant, the berry and the thorns'. What did it mean? (3)

8. Based on what you have read, do you think the boy's father will keep his promise to turn over a new leaf? (4)

40 Marks

Paper 2, Comprehension B

Answer the questions on the newspaper article printed below:

Hologram Holidays And Calls To The Cooker (*The Times* 7/1/84)
Peter Waymark

1 You wake up in the morning to a cup of tea, your favourite radio programme—and the bath water, already run and waiting for you at precisely the temperature you programmed the night before. You get dressed and have breakfast and set out for the office.

2 It is unlikely, however, that you will be crawling through traffic or waiting on a crowded platform for the 8.15. The office is probably only a couple of yards from where you had your egg and bacon (or the synthetic equivalent) but still equipped for your every need.

3 There will be a telephone, of course, but linked to a screen so that you can see (and be seen) by the person you have called; a business conference can be conducted over hundreds of miles, if not continents. You will have a facsimile machine, capable of transmitting exact copies of documents, charts, computer printouts and detailed drawings across the world within seconds.

4 Letters need not be put into envelopes, stamped and taken to the post office. An electronic mail system will take care of that: the message is written at your computer terminal and transmitted, along telephone line or cable, to a central mailbox which the recipient 'opens' by keying in his or her name and pass number.

5 While the breadwinner is thus busy, the household manager (male or female) will be sitting in an armchair with a keypad—very much like the present remote control for a television set—and a portable visual display. He or she will be setting programmes for the day or perhaps days and weeks ahead.

6 The central heating, for instance: temperatures can be set for each room in the house, and hour by hour throughout the day. You can arrange for the washing machine to come on at a certain time, or the cooker or the extractor fan. Light switches will be a thing of the past since lights can be programmed to switch on and off automatically, their brightness or dimness also centrally controlled.

7 You do not even need to be in the house. If you are on holiday and want to make sure that the house will be warm on your return, you can send instructions to the central heating boiler down the telephone line. Similarly if you left the casserole in the oven but forgot to turn the power on, a telephone call to the cooker will put things right.

8 The combination of sensors which can pick up information, microchips which can store it and optical fibre cables little fatter than a human hair which can carry it across continents are already revolutionizing the way we live; and the process can only accelerate.

9 Not every 1994 house will have every feature described here. What we are suggesting is the likely shape of things to come, based on forecasts from technology that is either already available or about to be developed. In the end it will depend on price and, most important, whether the public actually wants what it is offered.

10 In many cases the facilities for making life easier will surely overcome any doubts. Why make a special journey to the bank, when, at the behest of a keyboard precise details of the state of your account can be called up on a screen and you can pay in and withdraw money without a pen touching paper?

11 Shopping, too, will become a simple matter of calling up your supermarket on the visual display, finding out what items are available at what prices, even being able to see them. You key in your shopping list, the shop collects and packs the goods for you, debits your bank account and you call round at your convenience.

12 You fancy an evening at the theatre. You call up the relevant page on your viewdata system, telling you what shows are on. You choose one, key into the theatre where it is playing and find out performance times, availability of tickets and prices. You make your choice, give your credit number and in seconds the deal is done.

13 You can book a holiday in the same way, telling the travel agent where and when you want to go and how much you want to spend and back will come the information on your screen. You may also be able to see a short film of the resort to help you make up your mind.

14 It will be possible not only to watch the television screen but to write on it, transmitting the drawing or graphics via telephone line or cable and simultaneously carrying on a conversation with someone miles away. This will have important implications for education, putting teacher and pupil in direct contact without either being in a classroom.

15 Video, too, will take on an increasingly educational role. By 1994 the videodisc will surely have acquired the ability to record, as well as

play, and once it does the videocassette may be left for dead. In any case, the disc is a more effective and versatile means of storing information.

16 Not only will it be able to provide a complete course in chemistry or car maintenance but it will also be 'interactive', asking and answering questions. Your car engine fails to start. You slot in a disc and look for the relevant page in the index. The programme comes up with a set of propositions, that the battery is flat, the plugs are damp, you have run out of fuel. You respond, receive further information and eventually the cause of your problem should be discovered.

17 Television will still be there in 1994, and so will the BBC and IBA whose charters will have a couple of years to run. But cable and satellite will be well established, giving a choice of perhaps 30 channels. The viewer will be able to tune into the latest feature film and live coverage of a sporting event on the other side of the world, as well as picking up local news down to parish council level.

18 Television will no longer be simply a piece of electronic wallpaper, unrolling an endless diet of soap operas and game shows. The key word, once more, is interactive, a two-way communication in which the viewer takes part. There might be a televised debate about a burning local issue. Householders would be asked for their views, face to television face, and a vote taken, the result of which would appear on the screen within seconds.

19 A high definition picture and a flat screen mounted on the wall will make watching television more like going to the cinema, perhaps reducing

cinemas themselves to a small number of specialized art houses. And by 1994 three dimensional television may just be starting to reach the home.

20 If it does, this will probably be the result of holography developing from the static 3D images of today to full moving pictures. A hologram is a type of photographic image, produced by a laser, which becomes three dimensional when light is projected on to it. Like a real object, it has depth and shows a different perspective when viewed from different angles.

21 The application of this to moving pictures transmitted to the home is one of the most exciting prospects for the next decade. Unlike the short-lived 3D movies of the early 1950s, holographic television should be watchable without spectacles and by allowing the viewer to look not just at the image but behind it, the effect should be far more realistic.

22 Meanwhile holograms will make their impact in the home in other ways. As the technology develops, so it will become feasible to have a hologram covering an entire wall. So the children's nursery could have a woodland scene, with trees and animals and Red Riding Hood's cottage, so true to life as to invite you to step inside; and the parents may have a sun-drenched Mediterranean beach to cheer up the winter.

23 The children, too, can have their wall-mounted television screen and they will be able to hear the successors to Duran Duran and Boy George through a system of natural sound transmitted neither stereophonically nor quadrophonically, but enveloping the whole room through ducts incorporated discreetly in the wall.

24 There will be electronic aids to learning as well as leisure. The door-to-door encyclopaedia salesman can happily be sent packing since several volumes can be carried on a single microchip. Homework will more likely consist of working out problems on a computer than memorizing facts or writing in exercise books.

25 Electronic toys will move from video games to robots. Instructions can be programmed through the computer or the robot will respond directly to commands given by the human voice. The robot can be educational, as well as a diversion, carrying a pen across a sheet of paper and tracing patterns which form a painless introduction to geometry.

26 There will be so many demands on visual displays and computers and keypads that they will be found in several rooms. At least they will make the house tidier. Instead of scruffy address books, full of names and telephone numbers half of which are out of date, such information can be put on to the computer and revised at regular intervals.

27 Remote monitoring through a screen may smack of Orwell's Big Brother but used to keep an eye (and an ear) on the baby in its cot upstairs, thanks to a camera in the nursery sending back signals, it has less sinister uses. And if a recalcitrant teenager defiantly goes on playing with his electronic gadgetry after he has been ordered to bed, the fact can be noted and the toy switched off.

28 Amid all this technology, however, some old-fashioned habits may survive. While it will be possible to store the complete works of Dickens, Jane Austen or, for that matter, Harold Robbins, on a tiny chip, our home of the future may need a room dedicated to the peaceful pursuit of reading paper-and-printing books. Or just contemplating the wonders of the natural, as opposed to the man-created world.

1. According to paragraphs 2 to 4, what will 'working in an office' be like in 1994? (5)

2. What will the household manager's job consist of? Look at paragraphs 5 to 7. (5)

3. How will technology make life easier according to the writer? Give your answer in the form of *notes* on the information supplied in paragraphs 10 to 16. (12)

4. How will television be different in ten years' time? (10)

5. What is a hologram? (3)

6. What entertainment and educational provisions for teenagers and children will be available in the home by 1994? (5)

40 Marks

Paper 1 Expression

Section A

A1 Grandparents
A2 Instant Power
A3 Three Houses

Section B

Essays

Paper 2 Understanding

Comprehension A:

Their Mother's Purse by Morley Callaghan

Comprehension B:

Give peace a chance

Paper 1, Section A

A1. Grandparents

*The poems and comments printed below are concerned with grandparents. Study them and discuss **SOME** of the points raised, adding points of your **own** in order to develop your arguments.*

Helen Paterson, age 14

'I enjoy going to see my grandparents. They always seem to have time to listen to me and they never criticize me in the way my parents do. They are always pleased to see me and they seem to appreciate any little job that I do for them.'

Susan Nicoll, age 11

'My nanny is always chatting. My grandad is a right misery. Between them they make a right pair.'

Mrs Hilton, age 72

'I have arthritis, so it's very difficult for me to get around these days. My daughter, who lives sixty miles away, has invited me to live with her family so that she can keep an eye on me. But I won't go! You see, my roots are here. I've lived here most of my life. Besides there's some truth in the old saying, "Familiarity breeds contempt".'

Mr Ashton, age 67

'Many of us are rejected when we are old. Younger, active people say that we are slow, old fashioned and out of date. So they leave us to our memories and hours of loneliness. It is true that we can't get around quickly any more, but I think that we still have a lot to offer. We have the wisdom and experience that comes from a long life. But even more importantly, in an age where people do so much rushing around, we have the time to sit and listen.'

Kevin Brown, age 12

'Grandparents live in their own funny world where time seems to go backwards.'

Susan Legg, age 15

'She sits there living,
In her memories,
The young men, the laughter,
The river boats,
Summer teas and romance.
Romance unlike any other,
Special, strong and
Everlasting.'

(Children's remarks taken from *Grandmas and Grandpas*, ed. Richard and Helen Exley)

Paper 1, Section A

A2. Instant Power

Read the extract below and use it as a basis for your answer to ONE of the questions which follow. You may add extra details if you wish.

If your writing is average size (7 words to the line) then your answer should take up about 25 lines of your answer book. If you write a letter, its body should be not less than 18 lines of average size writing, and it should be properly set out.

Write appropriately and organise your material well. In this question the main emphasis is on clear, concise and logical explanation.

Extract from *The Hemsley Courier* Friday, 27:9:84

INSTANT POWER SCHEME GIVEN GO AHEAD

The 'Instant Power' scheme is all set to take off in Hemsley.

The idea is for young, unemployed people to form their own business and sell their combined skills to the public —tackling the sorts of jobs people have always meant to do but have not had time for.

Under the umbrella of Hemsley Borough Council, local industrial, voluntary and statutory organisations are to be invited to support the setting up of an instant power group with financial and practical help and advice.

Youth leader, Mrs Maxine Withers, who is acting as co-ordinator of the scheme, has called a meeting for next Wednesday at Hemsley Civic Hall. At the meeting details of the scheme are to be discussed by representatives of 18 organisations in the town.

Mrs Withers hopes that four or five people, experienced in the business world, will come forward to examine the market potential of the available skills and produce a business plan.

'It is vital to combine the experience of older people with the energy of the younger ones,' she said.

The next step will be to set up the group in suitable premises, provide it with tools, materials and a vehicle, and give it financial backing until such time as it is able to stand on its feet.

(a) Write a letter to Mrs Withers applying to join the Instant Power Scheme and giving details of your qualifications.

(b) As a rate-payer in Hemsley, write a letter to *The Hemsley Courier*, expressing your views on the proposal to use public funds to set up and underwrite the Instant Power scheme.

(c) Write an article for inclusion in next Friday's edition of *The Hemsley Courier* giving details of the proceedings and decisions made at the Wednesday meeting of the local organisations' representatives and interested members of the public.

(d) Write a letter, which could be copied and circulated, from Mrs Withers to the heads of business, voluntary and statutory organisations in Hemsley, describing the Instant Power scheme and asking for their support.

(e) You are a skilled tradesperson in his/her mid-forties who has been made redundant. Write a letter to Mrs Withers, expressing your interest in the scheme, and offering your services.

(f) Design a one-page leaflet advertising the services offered by Instant Power. The leaflet should provide full details of the scheme, since it will be sent to prospective customers.

Paper 1, Section A

A3. Three Houses

Study the drawings of these three living-rooms.

Describe each one, pointing out their similarities and differences. Then say which of these rooms you prefer, giving your reasons.

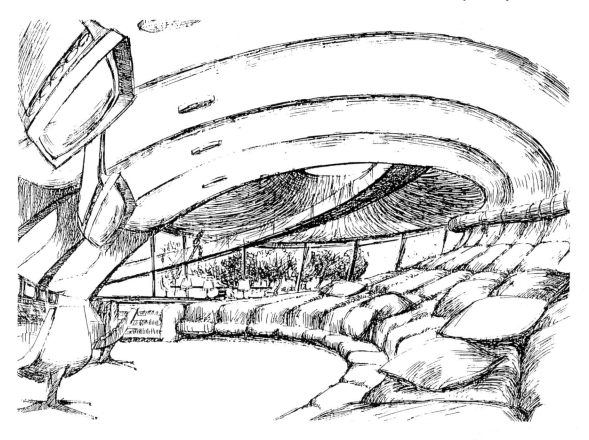

Paper 1, Section B

*Write about two sides on **ONE** of the following. You should aim to produce an imaginative and lively piece of writing.*

B1.

You can put up with quite a bit Tuesday, but it might be useful to jog someone's memory that it's time you got	a bit of praise and adulation for what you've done for them. You're as patient as Job today.'

These were your 'stars' in the daily newspaper yesterday. Write a story illustrating *either* how wrong *or* how right they were.

B2. What makes people laugh?

B3. Imagine that you played a key role in a major event in history. Decide on the role you played and describe the event.

B4. Saturdays.

B5. Write a story which illustrates the saying 'to burn the candle at both ends'.

B6. You have been asked to cook for twenty cubs or brownies at their annual camp. Describe the experiences you had producing your first meal for them.

B7. Read the following extract from a newspaper article. Then write about DIVORCE in any way you like.

'How do children cope with the trauma of divorce? Last week a report revealed that in America older children are emotionally scarred for life and it takes younger ones ten years to overcome fear and the sense of abandonment. But a British survey of 100 London children argues that it is not necessarily a bad experience.	There are, say authors Yvette Walczak and Sheila Burns, four distinct types of children of divorced parents: Those who feel they have suffered badly; those who feel they have not been affected at all; those who have mixed feelings; and those who feel the divorce has improved their lives.'

B8. My triumph.

B9. Describe a holiday you have spent in EITHER a tent OR a caravan OR on a boat.

B10. Study the photograph and write about it in any way you like.

Paper 2, Comprehension A

Read the short story below and then answer the questions which follow.

Their Mother's Purse by **Morley Callaghan** from Short Stories (MacGibbon & Kee)

Joe went around to see his mother and father, and while he was talking with them and wondering if he could ask for the loan of a dollar, his sister Mary, who was dressed to go out for the evening, came into the room and said, 'Can you let me have fifty cents tonight, Mother?'

She was borrowing money all the time now, and there was no excuse for her, because she was a stenographer[1] and made pretty good pay. It was not the same with her as it was with their older brother, Stephen, who had three children, and could hardly live on his salary.

'If you could possibly spare it, I'd take a dollar,' Mary was saying in her low and pleasant voice as she pulled on her gloves. Her easy smile, her assurance that she would not be refused, made Joe feel resentful. He knew that if he had asked for money, he would have shown that he was uneasy and a little ashamed, and that his father would have put down his paper and stared at him and his mother would have sighed and looked dreadfully worried, as though he were the worst kind of spend-thrift.

Getting up to find her purse, their mother said, 'I don't mind lending it to you, Mary, though I can't figure out what you do with your money.'

'I don't seem to be doing anything with it I didn't use to do,' Mary said.

'And I seem to do nothing these days but hand out money to the lot of you. I can't think how you'll get along when I'm dead.'

'I don't know what you'd all do if it weren't for your mother's purse,' their father said, but when he spoke he nodded his head at Joe, because he would rather make it appear that he was angry with Joe than risk offending Mary by speaking directly to her.

'If anybody wants money, they'll have to find my purse for me,' the mother said. 'Try and find it, Mary, and bring it to me.'

Joe had always thought of Mary as his young sister, but the inscrutable expression he saw on her face as she moved around the room picking up newspapers and looking on chairs made him realize how much more self-reliant, how much apart from them, she had grown in the last few years. He saw that she had become a handsome woman. In her tailored suit and felt hat, she looked almost beautiful, and he was suddenly glad she was his sister.

By this time his mother had got up and was trying to remember where she had put the purse when she came in from the store. In the way of a big woman, she moved around slowly, with a far-away expression in her eyes. The purse was a large, black, flat leather purse, but there never had been a time when his mother had been able to get up and know exactly where her purse was, though she used to pretend she was going directly to the spot where she had placed it.

Now she had got to the point where her eyes were anxious as she tried to remember. Her husband, making loud clucking noises with his tongue, took off his glasses and said solemnly, 'I warn you, Mrs McArthur, you'll lose that purse some day, and then there'll be trouble and you'll be satisfied.'

---

[1] *stenographer:* shorthand typist

She looked at him impatiently, as she had hunted in all the likely corners and cupboards. 'See if you can find my purse, will you, son?' she begged Joe, and he got up and began to help, as he used to do when he was a little boy. Because he remembered that his mother sometimes used to put her purse under the pillow on her bed, he went to look in the bedroom. When he got to the door, which was half closed, and looked in, he saw Mary standing in front of the dresser with their mother's purse in her hands. He saw at once that she had just taken out a bill and was slipping it into her own purse—he even saw that it was a two-dollar bill. He ducked back into the hall before she could catch sight of him. He felt helpless and knew only that he couldn't bear that she should see him.

Mary, coming out of the bedroom, called, 'I found it. Here it is, Mother.'

'Where did you find it, darling?'

'Under your pillow.'

'Ah, that's right. Now I remember,' she said, and looked at her husband triumphantly, for she never failed to enjoy finding the purse just when it seemed to be lost forever.

As Mary handed the purse to her mother, she was smiling, cool, and unperturbed, yet Joe knew she had put the two dollars into her own purse. It seemed terrible that she was able to smile and hide her thoughts like that when they had all been so close together for so many years.

'I never have the slightest fear that it's really lost,' the mother said, beaming. Then they watched her, as they had watched her for years after she had found her purse; she was counting the little roll of bills. Her hand went up to her mouth, she looked thoughtful, she looked down into the depths of the purse again, and they waited almost eagerly, as if expecting her to cry out suddenly that the money was not all there. Then, sighing, she took out fifty cents, handed it to Mary, and it was over, and they never knew what she thought.

'Good night, Mother. Good night, Dad,' Mary said.

'Good night, and don't be late. I worry when you're late.'

'So long, Joe.'

'Just a minute,' Joe called, and he followed Mary out to the hall. The groping, wondering expression on his mother's face as she counted her money had made him feel savage.

He grabbed Mary by the arm just as she was opening the door.

'Wait a minute,' he whispered.

'What's the matter, Joe? You're hurting my arm.'

'Give that bill back to them. I saw you take it.'

'Joe, I needed it.' She grew terribly ashamed and couldn't look at him. 'I wouldn't take it if I didn't need it pretty bad,' she whispered.

They could hear their father making some provoking remark, and they could hear the easy, triumphant answer of their mother. Without looking up, Mary began to cry a little; then she raised her head and begged in a frightened whisper, 'Don't tell them, Joe. Please don't tell them.'

'If you needed the money, why didn't you ask them for it?'

'I've been asking for a little nearly every day.'

'You only look after yourself, and you get plenty for that.'

'Joe, let me keep it. Don't tell them, Joe.'

Her hand tightened on his arm as she pleaded with him. Her face was now close against his, but he was so disgusted with her he tried to push her away. When she saw that he was treating her as though she were a cheap crook, she looked helpless and whispered, 'I've got to do something. I've been sending money to Paul Farrel.'

'Where is he?'

'He's gone to a sanitarium, and he had no money,' she said.

In the moment while they stared at each other, he was thinking of the few times she had brought Paul Farrel to their place, and of the one night when they had found out that his lung was bad. They had made her promise not to see him any more, thinking it was a good thing to do before she went any further with him.

'You promised them you'd forget about him,' he said.

'I married him before he went away,' she said. 'It takes a lot to look after him. I try to keep enough out of my pay every week to pay for my lunches and my board here, but I never seem to have enough left for Paul, and then I don't know what to do.'

'You're crazy. He'll die on your hands,' he whispered. 'Or you'll have to go on keeping him.'

'He'll get better,' she said. 'He'll be back in maybe a year.' There was such an ardent fierceness in her words, and her eyes shone with such eagerness, that he didn't know what to say to her. With a shy, timid smile, she said, 'Don't tell them, Joe.'

'O.K.,' he said, and he watched her open the door and go out.

He went back to the living-room, where his mother was saying grandly to his father, 'Now you'll have to wait till next year to cry blue ruin.'

His father grinned and ducked his head behind his paper. 'Don't worry. There'll soon be a next time,' he said.

'What did you want to say to Mary?' his mother asked.

'I just wanted to know if she was going my way, and she wasn't,' Joe said.

And when Joe heard their familiar voices and remembered Mary's frightened, eager face, he knew he would keep his promise and say nothing to them. He was thinking how far apart he had grown from them; they knew very little about Mary, but he never told them anything about himself, either. Only his father and mother had kept on going the one way. They alone were still close together.

Their Mother's Purse by **Morley Callaghan**

1. Why had Joe and Mary come to visit their parents?   (1)

2. Using the evidence in paragraphs 3 and 4 what differences are there in the parents' attitudes to Mary and to Joe?   (5)

3. How did Joe's opinion of Mary change during the course of the story?   (5)

4. What kind of person does the mother seem to be? Give evidence to support your ideas.   (10)

5. EITHER

(a) What do you think of Mary's motives for stealing from her mother?

OR

(b) Do you think Joe was right to say nothing?

In both cases give reasons for your opinions.   (4)

6. At the end of the story, Joe noticed that:

'Only his father and mother had kept on going the one way.
They alone were still close together.'

What do you think he meant by this? (3)

7. Imagine Mary's parents discovered their daughter's theft.
What would they say to her, and what would she say to them?
Describe such an occasion. (12)

40 Marks

OR

(b) Write an imaginary letter from Mary to her secret husband Paul
in the sanitorium. Date it *after* the incidents recounted
in the story. (12)

40 Marks

Paper 2, Comprehension B

Answer the questions on the newspaper article printed below:

All They Are Saying Is Give Peace A Chance Susan Tirbutt (*The Guardian* 3/1/84)

The noise made it difficult for anyone to be heard: a class of 28 girls talking at each other. None listening; each seeming
5. to compete to drown another's words. Second form peace studies at Notre Dame High School, Elephant and Castle, was in full voice.
10. Deliberately so. The exercise asking 12 and 13-year-olds to talk at each other for a minute and then questioning how they had felt
15. about it was designed as a lesson in the value of listening.
Given in a classroom decorated with fabrics of doves and anti-war posters
20. announcing violence ends where love begins and war no more, the weekly lesson is one element in the school's inte-grated approach to peace
25. studies.
Highlighting the only row, an artificial one at that, heard during a morning in a report of how one school seeks to
30. teach the relatively new school subject is much of the story. Peace has not excited most comment from historians, to judge by their published
35. works.
That perspective on the way history has been presented and perceived in schools, largely as a series of conflicts,
40. leaving an impression that war is natural and inevitable, is part of the thinking behind the school's peace studies policy.
Sister Myra Poole, head-
45. mistress, who started peace studies at Notre Dame 18 months ago as a result of dis-cussions in the Namur order of nuns to which she belongs,
50. sees it in the context of reinter-preting history.
Not that peace education is up there yet, she concedes. Reinterpreting the way
55. historical facts were seen is a conceptual development yet to come.
The young woman head of the school's history depart-

60. ment had herself only recently realised that history was not a long period of time punc-tuated by battles and kings, as she had been taught. At her
65. school nobody had tried to explain why they were doing anything. 'We just sat in lessons,' she said.
Her A level pupils at the 700
70. pupil Catholic girls com-prehensive are required by the needs of the examination system to learn a lot about 19th century politics and
75. warfare. The O level course is based on European and British political history.
CSE pupils, whose syllabus is designed by teachers in the
80. school, are studying the first world war. 'My aim is to get them to feel what it was like to be in the trenches. Looking at the whole waste of war in
85. terms of human rights.'
The peace message for the youngest pupils starts during daily 'guidance time' when their own occasional fights are
90. discussed.
Corporal punishment has never been used at the school, founded in 1855, according to Sister Anne-Marie, the
95. school's religious education teacher and first form tutor. Teachers try to show the pupils other ways of settling their arguments than by hit-
100. ting each other, mostly by talking and listening. They try to get them to acknowledge anger and why they feel it. This approach is carried
105. through the whole organisa-tion of the school, with the children encouraged to co-operate rather than compete. Prizes are awarded for effort,
110. not for academic success. Pupils are not placed com-petitively.
A railway track board game devised in the school to aid
115. cooperation shows a player that she will get further play-ing with another person and even further with another

three. The size of the board
120. makes the optimum number four.
Peace education, integrated throughout the curriculum, shows most obviously in
125. art—there are a lot of pictures of doves about the school—and religious education, where the intention is to present peace as an essential
130. element of the Christian message. The attitudes to life of other religions are aimed to be presented uncritically as part of the multi-cultural
135. policy in a school catering for pupils from 20 different national origins but of one religion.
In the less obvious areas,
140. such as geography, conflicts and their resolutions are explained by current examples, such as public planning inquiries presented
145. as a way of restricting conflict where there is a clash of interest.
Sport, which includes the conventional opposing team
150. games of hockey and netball, is the only area not directly affected by the peace ethos.
Direct teaching in the weekly peace slot is by a
155. member of the Teachers for Peace group, which is com-mitted to unilateral nuclear disarmament. Unusually, the post is graded as one of
160. responsibility.
The lesson for 12 and 13 year olds, on conflict, listen-ing and friendship, began with each girl introducing her
165. neighbour and saying some-thing about her. Most con-centrated on their neighbours' pets and brothers and sisters.
The pupils were then
170. launched into a minute of talking at each other, demon-strating the difficulty of simultaneous talking and listening against a noisy back
175. ground and how it makes people feel. They were then asked to form pairs, one

180. talking and one listening, grading each other and themselves as listeners. 'You think what it's like if *you* want to say something really important to someone, if you don't listen. Not really a
185. friend, are you?' asked their teacher.

Similar exercises are used in other classes when there is trouble between pupils. Each
190. is asked to write down something they like about everyone in the class, showing the pupils the positive qualities others like in them.
195. If the school's approach sounds all too soft and gentle, it is set in an often ungentle economic background. Opposite the War Museum
200. near London's Elephant and Castle, the school is in what would otherwise be regarded as a tough catchment area, tough because of low incomes
205. and high unemployment.

1. What is the purpose behind the exercise in which the class of 28 girls talk at each other?(2)

2. (a) Describe the way in which history has been taught in schools, according to the writer of this article. (3)

(b) How does Sister Myra Poole hope to change this perspective? (3)

(c) What had history lessons meant to the Head of History, when she was a schoolgirl?(2)

3. Why is the First World War being taught as part of the CSE syllabus? (3)

4. Describe the ways in which the school settles problems which arise between the girls. (10)

5. (a) Explain the meaning of 'integrated throughout the curriculum'. (Line 122) (2)

(b) Give evidence of the way in which peace studies are integrated. (8)

6. What do you learn from the article about the area the pupils come from? (3)

7. What would you say is the writer's purpose in this passage? Do you agree with what she has to say? Give your reasons. (4)

40 Marks

PAPER 1 EXPRESSION

Section A

A1 Organ Transplants

A2 Animal Experimentation

A3 Young People and Crime

Section B

Essays

PAPER 2 UNDERSTANDING

Comprehension A:

Her First Ball by Katherine Mansfield

Comprehension B:

Drugs

Paper 1, Section A

A1. Organ Transplants

*Below are printed several comments on the subject of transplanting organs from one body to another. Look at them carefully and then write an **essay** discussing **some** of the points raised. You may add some points of your own, but you should refer to some of those made here.*

A Religious Objector

'Transplanting organs is immoral and cannibalistic. It's against my religious beliefs! Besides it's too expensive.'

A Mother

'My son is only alive because of a transplant. I shall always be grateful to the parents who donated their dead son's kidney after a car crash. We still keep in touch.'

Doctor

'I think the public needs educating on the subject of transplanting organs from one body to another. Doctors don't tell the public enough. If the people knew more about it, I'm sure more of them would want to donate their kidneys or hearts to give other people a chance to live.'

Teenager

'Yes, I'm all for transplants, but preference should be given to young people.'

Transplant Lady

'It is five years since I had a transplant and I feel marvellous. Life has never been better.'

Parent

'It's so easy to say that transplants are wrong, but I know that if one of my children needed such an operation, I would consent and be eternally grateful to the donor.'

Member of Public

'I'm not at all sure about transplanting organs. Science is interfering with nature. Besides who is going to make the decisions about who should have a transplant and who shouldn't? Perhaps we should be spending the money on preventive medicine; teaching people how to eat and live a more healthy life.'

Paper 1, Section A

A2. Animal Experimentation

Read the extract below and use it as a basis for your answer to ONE of the questions which follow. You may add extra details if you wish. If your writing is average size (7 words to the line) then your answer should take up about 25 lines of your answer book. If you write a letter, its body should be not less than 18 lines of average size writing and it should be properly set out. Write appropriately and organize your material well. In this question the main emphasis is on clear, concise and logical explanation.

When they are opposed, scientists are always quick to defend the use of animals in research. Their main line of defence is to justify their experiments by telling us how their use of animals in research has led to miracle drugs, drugs which have wiped out many diseases. What they fail to tell us is that they also use animals as experimental subjects in a variety of other projects.

Some of these other projects include the testing of anti-riot devices, such as rubber bullets; the development of nerve gas and germ warfare, and using animals in space to test the effects of radiation, high rates of acceleration and weightlessness.

It is difficult to see how any of these experiments can benefit the human race. Using animals to discover ways of hurting people, for whatever reasons, is hard to justify.

Research scientists claim that if a product has been well and truly tested on animals, it should be safe for men, women and children. This line of defence is highly questionable. There are a tremendous number of differences between animals. What affects one animal does not affect another; what is safe for one is not safe for another. And so ultimately, no matter how much experimenting has been carried out, the first person who tries a new drug is the real guinea pig.

Although claims are made about drugs wiping out diseases, the whole subject of drugs is open to question. For instance, the side effects of some drugs can be dangerous, if not disastrous. Do you remember thalidomide? There are no guarantees that such disasters won't happen again, particularly with the rate at which drugs are produced today. Another aspect to consider with a degree of seriousness is the fact that big profits are reaped by drug companies!

Scientists, contrary to general public opinion, are not infallible. Like us, they are ordinary men and women. As such, they are capable of making mistakes. We suggest that animal experimentation is one of them.

Now write ONE of the following:

(a) Write *a letter* to your local newspaper protesting about the use of animals in experiments.

(b) Write *a speech* to be delivered to the press, in which you support the use of animals in experiments.

(c) Prepare *a leaflet* for the general public, protesting against the use of animals for experiments.

(d) As a scientist, answering the article and referring to the work in your laboratory, prepare *a report* for 'The British Union for the Abolition of Vivisection', justifying the use of animals in experiments.

(e) Write *a letter* to your M.P. asking him or her to speak in the House of Commons against all animal experiments. Provide information and suggest what might be included in the speech.

Paper 1, Section A

A3. **Young People and Crime**

Study the information given below about young people and crime. Write about your views on the subject, discussing possible causes of the problem and suggesting ways in which it might be overcome. Refer to some of the information provided and use additional information of your own.

These tables represent the crimes committed most frequently by all offenders (of all ages and both sexes).

MALE OFFENDERS found guilty of, or cautioned for indictable offences 1981

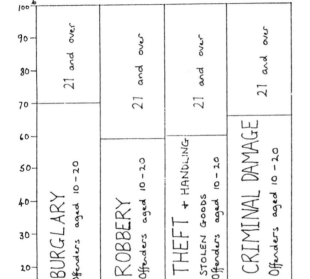

FEMALE OFFENDERS found guilty of, or cautioned for indictable offences 1981

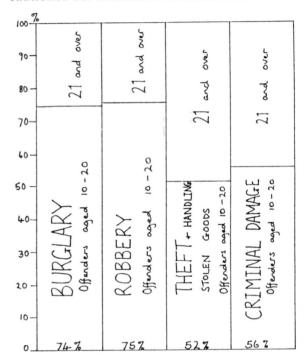

Persons received into custody on remand: by sex, age, verdict, and sentence, 1980

	England & Wales				Percentages and numbers			
	Males				Females			
	14–16	17–20	21 and over	All ages	14–16	17–20	21 and over	All ages
Found not guilty or not proceeded with	1	2	4	3	–	2	5	4
Found guilty								
Given a non-custodial sentence								
Absolute discharge	–	–	1	1	2	1	2	1
Conditional discharge	4	2	3	3	7	6	8	8
Probation order	–	8	6	7	3	22	14	17
Supervision order	4	–	–	–	10	–	.	–
Fine	3	6	8	7	1	7	8	8
Community service order	–	8	3	4	0	4	1	2
Care order	4	0		–	10	0	.	–
Suspended sentence	–	5	11	8	0	7	12	10
Other	9	4	5	5	8	8	10	9
Total given a non-custodial sentence	24	33	37	35	41	55	55	55
Given an immediate custodial sentence	71	56	47	52	51	27	26	27
Verdict/sentence not known	4	9	12	10	8	16	14	14
Total remanded in custody (= 100%) (numbers)	3,265	17,198	29,878	50,341	100	1,332	2,264	3,696

Source: Home Office

(a) Over half the males found guilty of indictable offences in England and Wales in 1981 were under 21.

(b) In 1980, whilst 50,341 males were remanded in custody, only 3,696 females were.

(c) The offence rate amongst females, although lower than for males, has risen considerably faster in the last twenty years.

(d) In 1981, the proportions of female offenders aged 10 to 13, and 14 to 16, dealt with by cautioning (as opposed to a non-custodial or a custodial sentence) were 87% and 60% respectively.

(e) In the same year, the proportions of male offenders aged 10 to 13, and 14 to 16, dealt with by cautioning were 68% and 34% respectively.

(f) The proportions of male offenders, under the age of 21, who are reconvicted of crime within two years of their release from custody are as follows:

Detention centres	63%
Borstal	68%
Prison	69%

Paper 1, Section B

Choose ONE of the following subjects for composition.

B1. Discuss the attractions of adventure holidays for young people.

B2. Before deciding on a career *either* in nursing *or* in the care of the old *or* in a leisure centre, you decide to do some voluntary work in that area.

Describe how this experience *either* makes you determined to pursue this kind of work *or* makes you change your mind.

B3. Do you think that teenagers today are irresponsible and undisciplined?

B4. Why is 'pop' music so popular?

B5. What are your views on the subject of surrogate motherhood?

B6. Every large town and city should have a leisure centre. Give your views on this statement, assessing the benefits to the community as a whole which such a centre would provide.

B7. Write a letter to a friend giving him or her advice on interviewing techniques.

B8. Sometimes after a crime which has caught the interest of the public, certain people make large sums of money from giving newspaper interviews. How do you feel about this?

B9. To what extent do you think our physical appearance affects our whole personality?

B10.

IRELAND. . .the problem goes on and on. From television we get one viewpoint. We can see the streets, and the soldiers in combat gear, running to their next cover. But the reality is always at a distance. It takes a book like 'Contact,' by A.F.N. Clarke (Pan, £1.75) to let us smell the sweat and the cordite, feel the fear, hear the crack of unexpected rifle fire. It is a blockbuster of a book, not for the squeamish. It is too real for that. Tony Clarke served with the Parachute Regiment for seven years and did two tours in Ulster.

His first tour, in 1973, came at a particularly tense time. The British Government were being criticised for their policy, the RUC no longer patrolled large areas of Belfast, and 3 Para were being accused of brutality.

'The Parachute Regiment had quite a lot of flak thrown at it from all angles, but we were trained killers. All our working moments were spent to that end,' says Tony Clarke. 'Is it safer for soldiers to get shot or to go in hard and be brutal? We didn't lose a man then.'

'Contact' tells the story from the soldier's point of view. It is written out of anger and the seeming acceptance that all this can be happening in a British city.

This is a book review.

Write a review, but at greater length, about any book which caught your interest and which you feel would interest others.

Paper 2, Comprehension A

Read the short story below and then answer the questions which follow.

Her First Ball by Katherine Mansfield

Exactly when the ball began Leila would have found it hard to say. Perhaps her first real partner was the cab. It did not matter that she shared the cab with the Sheridan girls and their brother. She sat back in her own little corner of it, and the bolster on which her hand rested felt like the sleeve of an
5. unknown young man's dress suit; and away they bowled, past waltzing lamp-posts and houses and fences and trees.

'Have you really never been to a ball before, Leila? But, my child, how too weird—' cried the Sheridan girls.

'Our nearest neighbour was fifteen miles,' said Leila softly, gently opening
10. and shutting her fan.

Oh dear, how hard it was to be indifferent like the others! She tried not to smile too much; she tried not to care. But every single thing was so new and exciting. . .Meg's tuberoses, Jose's long loop of amber, Laura's little dark head, pushing above her white fur like a flower through snow. She would
15. remember for ever. It even gave her a pang to see her cousin Laurie throw away the wisps of tissue paper he pulled from the fastenings of his new gloves. She would like to have kept those wisps as a keepsake, as a remembrance. Laurie leaned forward and put his hand on Laura's knee.

'Look here, darling,' he said. 'The third and the ninth as usual. Twig?'
20. Oh, how marvellous to have a brother! In her excitement Leila felt that if there had been time, if it hadn't been impossible, she couldn't have helped crying because she was an only child and no brother had ever said 'Twig?' to her; no sister would ever say, as Meg said to Jose that moment, 'I've never known your hair go up more successfully than it has to-night!'
25. But, of course, there was no time. They were at the drill hall already; there were cabs in front of them and cabs behind. The road was bright on either side with moving fan-like lights, and on the pavement gay couples seemed to float through the air; little satin shoes chased each other like birds.

'Hold on to me, Leila; you'll get lost,' said Laura.
30. 'Come on, girls, let's make a dash for it,' said Laurie.

Leila put two fingers on Laura's pink velvet cloak, and they were somehow lifted past the big golden lantern, carried along the passage, and pushed into the little room marked 'Ladies'. Here the crowd was so great there was hardly space to take off their things; the noise was deafening. Two benches on either
35. side were stacked high with wraps. Two old women in white aprons ran up and down tossing fresh armfuls. And everybody was pressing forward trying to get at the little dressing-table and mirror at the far end.

A great quivering jet of gas lighted the ladies' room. It couldn't wait; it was dancing already. When the door opened again and there came a burst of
40. tuning from the drill hall, it leaped almost to the ceiling.

Dark girls, fair girls were patting their hair, tying ribbons again, tucking handkerchiefs down the fronts of their bodices, smoothing marble-white gloves. And because they were all laughing it seemed to Leila that they were all lovely.

45. 'Aren't there any invisible hairpins?' cried a voice. 'How most extraordinary! I can't see a single invisible hairpin.'

'Powder my back, there's a darling,' cried someone else.

'But I must have a needle and cotton. I've torn simply miles and miles of the frill,' wailed a third.

50. Then, 'Pass them along, pass them along!' The straw basket of programmes was tossed from arm to arm. Darling little pink-and-silver programmes, with pink pencils and fluffy tassels. Leila's fingers shook as she took one out of the basket. She wanted to ask someone, 'Am I meant to have one too?' but she had just time to read: 'Waltz 3. *Two, Two in a Canoe*. Polka

55. 4. *Making the Feathers Fly*,' when Meg cried, 'Ready, Leila?' and they pressed their way through the crush in the passage towards the big double doors of the drill hall.

Dancing had not begun yet, but the band had stopped tuning, and the noise was so great it seemed that when it did begin to play it would never be heard.

60. Leila, pressing close to Meg, looking over Meg's shoulder, felt that even the little quivering coloured flags strung across the ceiling were talking. She quite forgot to be shy; she forgot how in the middle of dressing she had sat down on the bed with one shoe off and one shoe on and begged her mother to ring up her cousins and say she couldn't go after all. And the rush of longing she

65. had had to be sitting on the veranda of their forsaken up-country home, listening to the baby owls crying 'More pork' in the moonlight, was changed to a rush of joy so sweet that it was hard to bear alone. She clutched her fan, and, gazing at the gleaming, golden floor, the azaleas, the lanterns, the stage at one end with its red carpet and gilt chairs and the band in a corner, she

70. thought breathlessly, 'How heavenly; how simply heavenly!'

All the girls stood grouped together at one side of the doors, the men at the other, and the chaperones in dark dresses, smiling rather foolishly, walked with little careful steps over the polished floor towards the stage.

'This is my little country cousin Leila. Be nice to her. Find her partners;

75. she's under my wing,' said Meg, going up to one girl after another.

Strange faces smiled at Leila—sweetly, vaguely. Strange voices answered, 'Of course, my dear.' But Leila felt the girls didn't really see her. They were looking towards the men. Why didn't the men begin? What were they waiting for? There they stood, smoothing their gloves, patting their glossy hair and

80. smiling among themselves. Then, quite suddenly, as if they had only just made up their minds that that was what they had to do, the men came gliding over the parquet. There was a joyful flutter among the girls. A tall, fair man flew up to Meg, seized her programme, scribbled something; Meg passed him on to Leila. 'May I have the pleasure?' He ducked and smiled. There came a dark

85. man wearing an eyeglass, then cousin Laurie with a friend, and Laura with a little freckled fellow whose tie was crooked. Then quite an old man—fat, with a big bald patch on his head—took her programme and murmured, 'Let me see, let me see!' And he was a long time comparing his programme, which looked black with names, with hers. It seemed to give him so much trouble

90. that Leila was ashamed. 'Oh, please don't bother,' she said eagerly. But instead of replying the fat man wrote something, glanced at her again. 'Do I remember this bright little face?' he said softly. 'Is it known to me of yore?' At this moment the band began playing; the fat man disappeared. He was tossed away on a great wave of music that came flying over the gleaming floor,

95. breaking the groups up into couples, scattering them, sending them spinning...

Leila had learned to dance at boarding school. Every Saturday afternoon the boarders were hurried off to a little corrugated iron mission hall where Miss Eccles (of London) held her 'select' classes. But the difference between

that dusty-smelling hall—with calico texts on the walls, the poor, terrified
100. little woman in a brown velvet toque with rabbit's ears thumping the cold
piano, Miss Eccles poking the girls' feet with her long white wand—and this,
was so tremendous that Leila was sure if her partner didn't come and she had
to listen to that marvellous music and to watch the others sliding, gliding over
the golden floor, she would die at least, or faint, or lift her arms and fly out
105. of one of those dark windows that showed the stars.

'Ours, I think —' Someone bowed, smiled, and offered her his arm; she
hadn't to die after all. Someone's hand pressed her waist, and she floated
away like a flower that is tossed into a pool.

'Quite a good floor, isn't it?' drawled a faint voice close to her ear.
110. 'I think it's most beautifully slippery,' said Leila.

'Pardon!' The faint voice sounded surprised. Leila said it again. And there
was a tiny pause before the voice echoed, 'Oh, quite!' and she was swung
round again.

He steered so beautifully. That was the great difference between dancing
115. with girls and men, Leila decided. Girls banged into each other and stamped
on each other's feet; the girl who was gentleman always clutched you so.

The azaleas were separate flowers no longer; they were pink and white flags
streaming by.

'Were you at the Bells' last week?' the voice came again. It sounded tired.
120. Leila wondered whether she ought to ask him if he would like to stop.

'No, this is my first dance,' said she.

Her partner gave a little gasping laugh. 'Oh, I say,' he protested.

'Yes, it is really the first dance I've ever been to.' Leila was most fervent.
It was such a relief to be able to tell somebody. 'You see, I've lived in the
125. country all my life up till now ...'

At that moment the music stopped and they went to sit on two chairs against
the wall. Leila tucked her pink satin feet under and fanned herself, while she
blissfully watched the other couples passing and disappearing through the
swing doors.
130. 'Enjoying yourself, Leila?' asked Jose, nodding her golden head.

Laura passed and gave her the faintest little wink; it made Leila wonder for
a moment whether she was quite grown up after all. Certainly her partner did
not say very much. He coughed, tucked his handkerchief away, pulled down
his waistcoat, took a minute thread off his sleeve. But it didn't matter. Almost
135. immediately the band started and her second partner seemed to spring from
the ceiling.

'Floor's not bad,' said the new voice. Did one always begin with the floor?
And then, 'Were you at the Neaves' on Tuesday?' And again Leila explained.
Perhaps it was a little strange that her partners were not more interested. For
140. it was thrilling. Her first ball! She was only at the beginning of everything.
It seemed to her that she had never known what the night was like before. Up
till now it had been dark, silent, beautiful very often—oh yes—but mournful
somehow. Solemn. And now it would never be like that again—it had opened
dazzling bright.
145. 'Care for an ice?' said her partner. And they went through the swing doors,
down the passage, to the supper-room. Her cheeks burned, she was fearfully
thirsty. How sweet the ices looked on little glass plates and how cold the
frosted spoon was, iced too! And when they came back to the hall there was
the fat man waiting for her by the door. It gave her quite a shock again to
150. see how old he was; he ought to have been on the stage with the fathers and
mothers. And when Leila compared him with her other partners he looked

shabby. His waistcoat was creased, there was a button off his glove, his coat looked as if it was dusty with French chalk.

'Come along, little lady,' said the fat man. He scarcely troubled to clasp
155. her, and they moved away so gently, it was more like walking than dancing. But he said not a word about the floor. 'Your first dance, isn't it?' he murmured.

'How *did* you know?'

'Ah,' said the fat man, 'that's what it is to be old!' He wheezed faintly as
160. he steered her past an awkward couple. 'You see, I've been doing this kind of thing for the last thirty years.'

'Thirty years?' cried Leila. Twelve years before she was born!

'It hardly bears thinking about, does it?' said the fat man gloomily. Leila looked at his bald head, and she felt quite sorry for him.
165. 'I think it's marvellous to be still going on,' she said kindly.

'Kind little lady,' said the fat man, and he pressed her a little closer and hummed a bar of the waltz. 'Of course,' he said, 'you can't hope to last anything like as long as that. No-o,' said the fat man, 'long before that you'll be sitting up there on the stage, looking on, in your nice black velvet. And
170. these pretty arms will have turned into little short fat ones, and you'll beat time with such a different kind of fan—a black ebony one.' The fat man seemed to shudder. 'And you'll smile away like the poor old dears up there, and point to your daughter, and tell the elderly lady next to you how some dreadful man tried to kiss her at the club ball. And your heart will ache,
175. ache'—the fat man squeezed her closer still, as if he really was sorry for that poor heart—'because no one wants to kiss you now. And you'll say how unpleasant these polished floors are to walk on, how dangerous they are. Eh, Mademoiselle Twinkletoes?' said the fat man softly.

Leila gave a light little laugh, but she did not feel like laughing. Was
180. it—could it all be true? It sounded terribly true. Was this first ball only the beginning of her last ball, after all? At that the music seemed to change; it sounded sad, sad; it rose upon a great sigh. Oh, how quickly things changed! Why didn't happiness last for ever? For ever wasn't a bit too long.

'I want to stop,' she said in a breathless voice. The fat man led her to the
185. door.

'No,' she said, 'I won't go outside. I won't sit down. I'll just stand here, thank you.' She leaned against the wall, tapping with her foot, pulling up her gloves and trying to smile. But deep inside her a little girl threw her pinafore over her head and sobbed. Why had he spoiled it all?
190. 'I say, you know,' said the fat man, 'you mustn't take me seriously, little lady.'

'As if I should!' said Leila, tossing her small dark head and sucking her underlip ...

Again the couples paraded. The swing doors opened and shut. Now new
195. music was given out by the bandmaster. But Leila didn't want to dance any more. She wanted to be home, or sitting on the veranda listening to those baby owls. When she looked through the dark windows at the stars they had long beams like wings ...

But presently a soft, melting, ravishing tune began, and a young man with
200. curly hair bowed before her. She would have to dance, out of politeness, until she could find Meg. Very stiffly she walked into the middle; very haughtily she put her hand on his sleeve. But in one minute, in one turn, her feet glided, glided. The lights, the azaleas, the dresses, the pink faces, the velvet chairs, all became one beautiful flying wheel. And when her next partner bumped her
205. into the fat man and he said, 'Par*don*,' she smiled at him more radiantly than ever. She didn't even recognize him again.

Her First Ball by **Katherine Mansfield**

1. How do we know that Leila regretted being an only child? (3)

2. Leila is so excited about going to her first dance. What evidence is there of her excitement between lines 25 and 57? (5)
('They were at the drill hall' ...... 'the big double doors of the drill hall.')

3. Describe what Leila's feelings had been as she was getting ready for the ball. (2)

4. 'But Leila felt the girls didn't really see her.' Line 77.
What do you think this means? (3)

5. (a) What are the young men like who dance with Leila? (3)

   (b) How do they contrast with Leila? (3)

6. The fat man says to Leila, 'Do I remember this bright little face?. . .Is it known to me of yore?' Lines 91 to 93.

   (a) What do you think he meant? (3)

   (b) Why does his conversation temporarily upset her? (4)

   (c) Why is the dance only temporarily spoilt for Leila to the extent that later on she doesn't even recognize him again? (3)

7. What evidence is there in this story to show that the setting is much earlier this century? (6)

8. Katherine Mansfield frequently uses language and images to evoke a feeling of excitement and anticipation as Leila attends her first ball. Provide evidence to support this statement. (5)

40 Marks

Paper 2, Comprehension B

Read the following article on drugs and then answer the questions.

A Generation On The Main Line To Tragedy by
Paul Brown (*The Guardian*,
3rd January, 1984)

Drug addicts are not just found collapsed in doorways in Piccadilly anymore. They are just as likely to be dis-
5. covered dancing the night away in provincial discos, and turning up late for work on Mondays. All over Britain through every class, in nearly
10. every town, it is fashionable if you are under 25 to smoke, snort, or inject yourself for kicks.

For most parents who
15. worry when their children have problems with school-work, or miss days at work, drug misuse is the last thing that crosses their minds. But
20. in 1984 a conscientious parent should check a teenager's eyeballs. If the pupils are unusually small or large it could be amphetamines or
25. heroin.

In both public schools and comprehensives these are the drugs now available. The young addicts have fallen in
30. love with the drugs that block out the reality of modern Britain—and they do not want their parents to interfere.

Detective Chief Inspector
35. Rex Woods, who has been dealing with drug problems in Bedfordshire for 15 years, says that Britain's parents—and the country's governing
40. class—have no understanding of the epidemic drugs prob-lem, nor of how to deal with it. 'When I was a schoolboy we were learning about girls
45. behind the bicycle sheds and experimented with Wood-bines and Players Weights.

Parents won't believe this, but now it's heroin and
50. amphetamines. People do not believe their children know about drugs, let alone try them. They should come down to Bury Park Road in
55. Luton and see the schoolgirls selling themselves so they can get a fix.'

Teenagers who get hooked have only two ways to raise
60. money for their habit—prosti-tution or stealing. Teenage boys recently arrested for drug offences in Luton had to have treatment for anal VD. Mr
65. Woods says that he and his squad are currently fighting a losing battle against the pushers. Alone, the police cannot hope to cope.
70. The picture he paints is a dismal one, but it depicts a pattern found repeated all over Britain. Drugs cut across all class barriers, and drag
75. down both addicts and their families.

A senior civil servant, an expert in his field, put it this way. 'We can never solve the
80. problem. Drugs will always be with us in some way or another, but we can do our best to minimise the effects.

We can do our best in
85. prevention by making the most of the Customs Service, and increasing the expertise and the manpower of the drugs squads in the police. We
90. can do everything we can to educate people so that they know the terrible risks they run and the damage they do themselves and other people.
95. We can give those people unfortunate enough to be addicted every chance of get-ting out of it by providing treatment, while accepting
100. that it is a chronic relapsing condition that requires sup-port from the rest of society and from voluntary organ-isations.'
105. The civil servant accepts that the Government is not doing any of these things. 'There is not,' he says, 'the political will.
110. Only when the electorate puts pressure on the Govern-ment to do something about it,' he says, 'will the problem be tackled with proper
115. energy.'

Talking to specialists in the field it is clear that most of the experts disagree with each other about the extent of the
120. problem, about how to tackle it and about who is to blame. With statistics and research in short supply, even 'the facts' are a matter of argument.
125. But they all agree that drug misuse in Britain is now at epidemic level, with the National Health Service unable to cope with the
130. thousands of addicts, and the customs and police failing to stop the flood of illegal drugs that is coming onto the market.
135. The number of addicts noti-fied to the Home Office is increasing 40 per cent a year, and there is evidence that the flow of drugs is now reaching
140. out from the cities to almost every town and housing estate. Reports of playground prostitution, so that school-girls can buy their next fix of
145. heroin, are by no means exaggerated. Yet very little is being said—and even less being done—to combat the problem.
150. The Department of Health has pledged to provide £6 million over three years for new initiatives to tackle the problem. The Home Secretary
155. is, among other measures, sending one Customs officer to Karachi to help stem the flow of heroin into Heathrow, and a policeman to Holland
160. to combat the cross Channel traffic. But in the meantime drugs worth more than £6 million are passing through Heathrow and Dover each
165. week, with carriers being paid £3,000 a time. At present they stand less than 1 per cent chance of being caught.

On the streets teenagers can
170. pick up heroin in £5 and £10 bags for what is now the most fashionable and cheapest way of getting 'stoned'. For many, 'smack' blocks out the reality
175. of teenage unemployment. Figures for Merseyside over the last three years give some

idea of the size of the problem. Seizures of heroin alone have gone up from five grammes in 1981 to 261 grammes in 1982, and 1,080 grammes in the first 10 months of 1983. The number of offenders has gone up from 12 to 286 in the same period.

The numbers actually hooked range from the official Home Office estimate of 40,000 to 50,000, to informed guesswork of researchers and agencies in the field which pushes it upwards to 100,000 or even 150,000.

The National Health Service, which is supposed to deal with the addicts who finally seek treatment, is still using a structure set up in the 1960s, to deal with the so-called explosion of drugs in that decade. Since then the problem has become more than 10 times as serious. Yet the resources devoted to it are roughly the same. In Chester, the one clinic with residential beds serving the whole of Merseyside has only six beds for heroin addicts.

On the waiting list for those beds are 80 heroin addicts between 18 and 22. All of them will have to wait at least three months before they have any hope of treatment. They are luckier than most. In many areas there are no facilities at all—and not likely to be.

The causes of the boom in the trade in illegal drugs in Britain, and the consequent leap in addiction, are complex. But they seem to combine unfortunate coincidence and apparent official indifference. While the public appears unconcerned about the problem, there is no pressure on the politicians to make tackling it a priority. Drug takers and the pushers become more entrenched.

Britain's bad luck stems from the sources of supply. In the late 1970s British hospitality to the middle classes fleeing Iran after the revolution meant we also received huge quantities of heroin. It was the easiest way of moving money out of Iran. The second supply boom, which is worsening all the time, originates in Pakistan—from the Afghan border.

Working on the bad luck theory alone, Britain would probably have been stuck with a drugs problem anyway. But many argue that official indifference, plus the side effects of Government policies, have made a poten-tially dangerous situation into a catastrophe.

First of all the Customs Service, the first line of defence against smuggling, was—while building up its special investigation branch —drastically cut back on uniformed officers. The police, while numbers have actually increased, have largely left their drugs squads unchanged. In many cases they have been used in other detective work. In other areas the National Health Service, social workers and voluntary organisations have had a total of £6 million pushed their way the last three years. But this seems unlikely to balance the resources already stripped away by Government cuts elsewhere.

In addition Government policies could be said to have created a group of potential addicts. Roger Lewis, one worker in the field, puts it like this: 'LSD was the drug of the sixties, it was supposed to expand the mind to take in the new horizons. Heroin is the drug of the 80s, it blocks out the pain and the hopelessness of unemployment and the bleakness of the future.'

1. According to the passage, where might drug addicts be found? (3)

2. Read lines 14 to 69.

('For most parents who worry. . .Alone, the police cannot hope to cope')
(a) How is a parent likely to know whether his child is a drug addict? (2)

(b) Why do young addicts turn to drugs? (2)

(c) How do many of them raise the money to buy drugs? (4)

3. Explain, using your own words as far as possible, what, according to a senior civil servant, can be done to stop the current trends in drug taking. (10)

4. What does the senior civil servant mean when he says 'There is not the political will'? Line 108. (2)

5. (a) What do the experts disagree on? (2)

(b) On what points do they agree? (3)

6. Read lines 195 to 219. ('The National Health .... and not likely to be')

Using your own words as far as possible, explain the reasons why it is difficult to treat addicts who ask for treatment. (4)

7. From line 221 ('The causes of the boom') to the end, the writer of the passage explores in general, and then in more detail, the reasons why there is a boom in the trade in illegal drugs in Britain. In a paragraph, say what he suggests are the causes. (8)

40 Marks

PAPER 1 EXPRESSION

Section A

A1 Changing fashions

A2 Health

A3 Charities

Section B

Essays

PAPER 2 UNDERSTANDING

Comprehension A:

A Sunrise on the Veld by Doris Lessing

Comprehension B:

Flight path to a good tip

Paper 1, Section A

A1. Changing Fashions

*The comments printed below are about different attitudes to fashion. Study them and discuss **some** of the points raised, adding points of your **own** to develop your arguments. You do not have to refer to all the points made below.*

Hairdresser's Apprentice
'I ignore fashion. I just do my own thing.'

Historian
'In the eighteenth century men in high society wore powdered wigs and cosmetics.'

Fourth Former
'My mother always makes me wear clothes of quality which will last. She just doesn't understand that I don't want clothes that last. Like my friends, I prefer to have lots of changes.'

Teenager
'Between you and me, I don't always like the clothes or shoes that I wear, but I know how people in my year at school make fun of anyone who doesn't wear fashionable things. It's easier to go along with what's expected of me. I wish we had to wear school uniform.'

Businessman
'People are so easily taken in. We dictate the fashions, they follow! One minute the public is into double glazing; the next minute split level cookers. At the moment en-suite bathrooms are the 'in' thing!'

Pensioner
'Young people nowadays are just exploited by commercial interests. New fads come and go at an alarming rate. We've had skate boarding, personal stereos, roller disco boots and B.M.X. bicycles. What will it be next, I wonder!'

Paper 1, Section A

A2. Health

Read the passages below.
*Write a **speech** for a young people's group, promoting good health. You should select the most important and effective points for your speech. You may add material of your own.*

Exercise

To be healthy we need exercise. This does not mean that we have to over-exercise or do anything which causes pain. In fact, exercise should be exhilarating and should help to prevent heart problems and obesity throughout our lives. Older people need exercise more than young children, who are constantly moving around. This list indicates some of the best activities for keeping our bodies in trim.

1. Swimming
2. Cycling
3. Gardening
4. Gymnastics
5. Disco Dancing
6. Squash

Diet

To be healthy we need to eat a well-balanced diet. This means that we need to eat a variety of food in the right quantities. Daily we need:

PROTEINS—which help digestion, are essential for body repair, maintenance and tissue growth. Young children need more than grown-ups. Cheese, meat, fish, eggs and milk are rich in protein.

CARBOHYDRATES—give us energy but if we eat too many carbohydrates, problems arise, since they are high in calories and have limited nutritional value. Sugar, bread, potatoes and rice are examples of carbohydrates.

VITAMINS—are found in fruit and vegetables. They are good for us. Care must be taken in cooking vegetables or vitamins are killed.

FIBRE—is necessary for the digestive system. It is vital to all of us but many of us do not have enough fibre in our diet. The following foods are rich in fibre—wholemeal bread, jacket potatoes, and certain cereals.

In addition to these we also need minerals and fats, in moderation.

The trouble is that most of us like the kinds of food which are not good for us, such as cakes, pastries, white bread and sugar. But if we remember the saying, 'Moderation in all things', and indulge in a treat occasionally, no real harm can be done to our bodies.

Addictions

To be healthy we need to make sure that we never become addicted to the following:

ALCOHOL—An occasional alcoholic drink will not harm us, but too much does! It affects the liver, our ability to judge speed and distance accurately, and it can cause severe headaches.

DRUGS—such as heroin, L.S.D., cannabis and amphetamines are addictive and can harm our bodies. Even tranquillisers and sleeping pills can affect our health if we take too many.

CAFFEINE—This is found in coffee and tea. It is a mild drug. If we take too much caffeine, it can affect our health by causing nervousness, tension and palpitations.

SMOKING—We cannot be healthy if we smoke. Smoking is a major cause of lung cancer, bronchitis and heart disease. In addition a pregnant woman can affect her baby by smoking.

Paper 1, Section A

A3. Charities

Here are a variety of facts, statistics and newspaper advertisements about:-

1. The N.S.P.C.C.

2. Christian Aid.

3. The Cancer Research Campaign.

*After studying the information carefully, write **an appeal** to a fund-raising group stating why the group should raise money for **one** of these charities, rather than for the other two.*

1. The N.S.P.C.C. 'The National Society for the Prevention of Cruelty to Children'

(a) The Society was formed just over 100 years ago. Since then, more than 9 million children have received help.

(b) Around 43,000 children receive help each year. Yes, even today! At least one child dies every week having been injured by parents. Others get burnt, bruised, neglected. Many simply lack love and affection.

(c) Money is desperately needed if the Society is to fulfil its obligations to go on caring for children in need.

(d) In its own words, here is what the Society would like to do if funds were available:

'We want to streamline all the work we do by bringing together our various activities and expertise—our inspectors, family centres, playgroups and special units—into a network of skilled Child Protection Teams working within the community and responding to *local* needs.

In this way we can provide a nationwide service of caring and counselling and respond even more efficiently and effectively to children and parents in need and to the very real problems they face today.

We aim to create 60 of these teams over the next five years, with the first ones in action by the end of 1984.

Because we believe that prevention really is better than cure, we want to strengthen our role as *preventers* of child abuse by identifying the causes and providing the facilities for dealing with them.

Above all we want to do everything possible to keep families together. Thankfully, thousands of parents actually come to us asking for help. We are *not* a prosecuting Society and very few of our cases come before the courts (though, uniquely for a voluntary body, we have the authority to take legal action on behalf of a child and use it if we think it necessary). Our ideal is to provide the means of improving the child's home life and encourage loving relationships between parents and children.'

The cruellest blow this child can receive now is for you to turn the page.

The damage has been done and what this child needs now is help. Like 43,000 children this year, she's relied on the NSPCC for that help. Now, in turn, we're looking to you. As an independent organisation, the NSPCC relies mainly on public donations.

Even if you can afford just 10p, you'll be paying for one of the 7,000 or more phone calls we have to make every day of the year (weekends and Bank Holidays included). If you send a larger donation you'll be helping us to set up one of our first child protection teams to provide 24 hour assistance to abused children and their families. Whatever you send it'll be used immediately to help children.

Helping to stem the flood of serious cases which we have to deal with every day. The NSPCC has been in existence for 100 years, during which time it's helped 9 million children.

To continue providing that help, we need you to send us a donation. Please send your donation to Dr. Alan Gilmour, NSPCC, Ref 49010 67 Saffron Hill, London EC1N 8RS.

And thank you for not turning over.

NSPCC. We've helped 9 million children in the last 100 years.

2. Christian Aid

(a) Each year, Christian Aid has a special collecting week, during May. 400,000 people volunteer to collect; many go from house-to-house.

(b) Christian Aid Week raises over £4.5 million out of a total income of £11 million.

(c) Administrative costs are kept as low as possible so that usually out of every £1 collected, 84p goes to help the poor.

(d) What happens to the money?

'In areas of poverty it is spent on agricultural instruction and demonstration, equipment, livestock, seeds, fertilisers, well-drilling, irrigation, settlement schemes, trade training, scholarships, and instruction in nutrition, hygiene, child welfare and community development. In short it is used to create opportunities for self-help. In emergencies it buys medical supplies, food, blankets, shelter and transport.'

(e) Who is helped?

'Those in greatest need, regardless of their religion or race. Christian Aid is so called because of its origins and motivation, but it asks nothing in return for the aid it gives and makes no distinction between Christian and non-Christian beneficiaries. It also helps those who suffer from natural disasters, wars and political oppression— whether that oppression is by black or white or by regimes of the right or the left.'

Dear Neighbour,

This note asks you to show you care about human suffering.

 The figure in this symbol represents the world's poor — deprived of opportunity and even of enough food, but determined to stand on their own feet with a minimum of help.

Here are some more symbols. They represent the sort of help most needed.

 FOOD — not free handouts but water supplies, better seed, better livestock and knowledge of better methods so that they can feed themselves and their communities.

 HEALTH — training and suitable medicines for local health workers, particularly where most people live far from towns with doctors and hospitals.

 SKILLS — training in breadwinning skills and trades for the landless and the town-dwellers who have to buy their food.

 ADVICE — to people who, unaware of their legal rights, are pushed off their land or exploited in other ways; and HELP to the dependants of those imprisoned without trial, tortured or killed for their views.

 SHELTER and RESETTLEMENT for refugees; also emergency food and medical supplies.

 And here's the symbol for what helps make these things possible: money. It's the most portable form of help — and most of us can afford to give at least some.

Christian Aid Week fundraising and publicity cost only 10p in the pound. The people to thank for this are your neighbours who collect donations and run fundraising events for your local Christian Aid committee. Please help make their voluntary efforts worthwhile.

Thank you.

For recorded news of current Christian Aid activities dial 01-733 0562

Christian Aid

240–250 Ferndale Rd, London SW9 8BH

3. Cancer Research Campaign

(a) Cancer kills just under 147,000 people in the United Kingdom every year. But as the facts below show, progress is being made all the time in preventing, controlling and curing cancer.

If you believe only a miracle can beat cancer, here's twenty.

To a lot of people the word 'cancer' is one of the most frightening in the English language.

They believe it's always incurable.

That it's the death sentence by another name.

And that the only thing they can do about it is hope for a miracle.

For many cancer sufferers, however, there is already far more than just hope.

Below you'll find evidence of the progress cancer research has made in recent years.

Of the many thousands to whom the word 'cancer' is no longer a death sentence.

And of the many areas of research now being successfully pursued.

Much remains to be done of course. (Especially since cancer does cause the death of nearly 147,000 people in this country every year.)

But as you'll see, cancer is being beaten.

1. As recently as 10 years ago, cancer killed hundreds of children every year. Now it's curable in 2 out of 3 cases.

2. One in ten of all cancers are skin cancer. Most are now entirely curable.

3. Forty years ago, doctors had no drug treatment to give cancer patients. Today there are over 30 effective anti-cancer drugs.

4. In the 1950's only 1 in 3 children with Hodgkin's disease survived. Since then the success rate has doubled.

5. The discovery of links between cigarette smoking and lung cancer has done much to persuade people not to smoke. And at last the deaths from lung cancer

Lorna Branczik was treated for cancer in 1971 and after three months was able to return to a full life.

are beginning to fall off.

6. Thirty years ago sufferers of testicular cancer had only a 50% survival rate. Today it's almost 90%.

7. The invention of the body scanner and its development during the 1970's has greatly improved the diagnosis and treatment of cancer.

8. Research has shown that 80% of cancers may be directly caused by our environment or life style, and therefore may be preventable.

9. Young people who would once have died from kidney cancer are now

usually able to make a full recovery.

10. The discovery of many cancer

Jenny Lockyer was treated for cancer 16 years ago. Today she leads an active normal life.

causing chemicals and materials, and the subsequent controls placed on them has greatly reduced the chances of getting cancer at work.

11. The introduction of cervical screening for women means that the risk of developing cancer of the cervix can be detected. And therefore, the disease is preventable.

12. Some hospitals now have specialist teams covering all aspects of cancer treatment, enabling patients to benefit from a greater range of expertise.

13. Not long ago 90% of all women with choriocarcinoma (cancer of the placenta) would have died. Today 90% recover.

14. Certain cancers of the ovary which occur in very young women were always fatal in the past. Now they are usually cured.

Eleven years ago, John Hill was told he had cancer. Today he is cured and leads a full family life.

15. The discovery of certain antibodies which home in on tumours has made it possible not only to locate otherwise hidden cancers but also to target anti-cancer drugs to destroy them.

16. Developments in radiotherapy have produced more accurate and more powerful machines which make the treatment both more acceptable and more effective.

17. Just five years ago scientists could only theorize about the innermost workings of cancerous cells. Today, new technology is enabling them to unravel the whole mystery.

18. Research has discovered that cancerous tumours often produce marker-substances in the body. These can be detected at a very early stage when the cancerous tumours can be eradicated.

19. Not only are doctors and scientists finding ways to cure cancer, they're also finding ways to ensure that the quality of life is subsequently undiminished.

20. In the past, cancer was almost inevitably a fatal disease. Today over 60,000 people are cured each year in Britain.

Of course, we at the Cancer Research Campaign cannot claim responsibility for all these developments.

They are the result of a worldwide campaign by many thousands of researchers and doctors.

Terry Mason was only eight when he developed cancer. Today he leads a normal schoolboy life.

However, as Britain's largest supporter of cancer research we do help finance over 600 projects throughout the country.

These cover everything from studying how cancer starts and how to prevent it, to developing new techniques for early detection and cure.

To continue these projects and start more, we need your contribution.

This can be either a donation through a deed of covenant, legacy or money.

Or a donation of your time in helping our local committees.

Over 92% of all the money we collect goes straight into research.

So however you can help us, you can be sure you'll be helping to give Britain's cancer sufferers a better chance.

Write to us now at Dept. TE1, 2 Carlton House Terrace, London SW1Y 5AR.

Or contact your local Cancer Research Campaign through the telephone directory.

The sooner you do, the sooner we'll be able to add another miracle.

Together, we can beat cancer.

Cancer Research Campaign

(b) It should be realised that cancer is not a single disease with a single cause. Doctors recognise some 200 types of cancer, each with different causes, affecting different parts of the body and responding differently to treatment.

(c) The nature of research is:

To find causes, so that cancers may be prevented.

To improve early detection and diagnosis.

To understand more about how and why cancer develops.

To find out new treatments and improve those that already exist.

To develop effective education about cancer for public, patients and health professionals.

Paper 1, Section B

Choose one of the following subjects for composition.

B1. Account for the rapidly growing popularity of the video.

B2. To what extent do you think that the first five years of our lives are important in determining what kind of people we turn out to be?

B3. The National Trust.

B4. Forgiveness forgotten

'I was interested to read that the Church of Scotland has refused to allow a convicted murderer into its ministry, even though he has finished his prison sentence and come to Christian faith and commitment.

Do the leaders of the Kirk realise that their attitude would prevent Moses and St Paul from being Ministers of the Church of Scotland?

The Bible teaches a doctrine of God's full and free forgiveness; the blood of Jesus Christ, His Son, purifies us from every sin (1 John 1:7).'
(Rev) DAVID J BLAKE, Stafford

What are your feelings on this subject?

B5. What qualities make a good youth leader?

B6. What do you think are the main causes of soccer hooliganism and what would you do to reduce it?

B7. The advantages and disadvantages of living on a new housing estate.

B8. 'I CAN'T help feeling we have rather muddled loyalties. Horrific scenes of IRA bombings or the wars in the Lebanon are seen on television without people so much as batting an eyelid. But bring on a lost dog or homeless donkey, or show horses falling in the Grand National, and you have them ringing the TV studios, jamming the switchboards with offers of money and homes.

I know most animals are cute and cuddly and I've got nothing against them or the RSPCA but people should open their eyes to what is happening in the real world.'
MARY EMMET (17)
Cropston, Leicestershire

Do you think, as this letter suggests, that, as a race, the British are more concerned about what happens to animals than what happens to people at home or abroad?

B9. Many pupils and students have part-time jobs at weekends and in the evenings. What are the advantages and disadvantages of part-time work?

B10. Poor learners

'I think it very unfair that while 16-year-olds who have left school and are unable to get a job receive dole money, others who stay on at school to better their education receive nothing.

Don't all 16-year-olds have similar needs—clothes, money for discos, football matches and so on?'
MARK HURTON (16)
Barton-upon-Humber
S. Humberside

What are your views on this subject?

Paper 2, Comprehension A

Read the short story below and then answer the questions which follow.

A Sunrise On The Veld by **Doris Lessing,** from 'This was the Old Chief's Country' (Michael Joseph) © 1951, Doris Lessing

Every night that winter he said aloud into the dark of the pillow: Half past four! Half past four! till he felt his brain had gripped the words and held them fast. Then he fell asleep at once, as if a shutter had fallen; and lay with his face turned to the clock so that he could see it first thing when he woke.

5. It was half past four to the minute, every morning. Triumphantly pressing down the alarm-knob of the clock, which the dark half of his mind had out-witted, remaining vigilant all night and counting the hours as he lay relaxed in sleep, he huddled down for a last warm moment under the clothes, playing with the idea of lying abed for this once only. But he played with it for the

10. fun of knowing that it was a weakness he could defeat without effort; just as he set the alarm each night for the delight of the moment when he woke and stretched his limbs, feeling the muscles tighten, and thought: Even my brain—even that! I can control every part of myself.

Luxury of warm rested body, with the arms and legs and fingers waiting

15. like soldiers for a word of command! Joy of knowing that the precious hours were given to sleep voluntarily!—for he had once stayed awake three nights running, to prove that he could, and then worked all day, refusing even to admit that he was tired; and now sleep seemed to him a servant to be com-manded and refused.

20. The boy stretched his frame full-length, touching the wall at his head with his hands, and the bedfoot with his toes; then he sprung out, like a fish leaping from water. And it was cold, cold.

He always dressed rapidly, so as to try and conserve his night-warmth till the sun rose two hours later; but by the time he had on his clothes his hands

25. were numbed and he could scarcely hold his shoes. These he could not put on for fear of waking his parents, who never came to know how early he rose.

As soon as he stepped over the lintel, the flesh of his soles contracted on the chilled earth, and his legs began to ache with cold. It was night: the stars were glittering, the trees standing black and still. He looked for signs of day,

30. for the greying of the edge of a stone, or a lightening in the sky where the sun would rise, but there was nothing yet. Alert as an animal he crept past the dangerous window, standing poised with his hand on the sill for one proudly fastidious moment, looking in at the stuffy blackness of the room where his parents lay.

35. Feeling for the grass-edge of the path with his toes, he reached inside another window farther along the wall, where his gun had been set in readiness the night before. The steel was icy, and numbed fingers slipped along it, so that he had to hold it in the crook of his arm for safety. Then he tiptoed to the room where the dogs slept, and was fearful that they might have been

40. tempted to go before him; but they were waiting, their haunches crouched in reluctance at the cold, but ears and swinging tails greeting the gun ecstatically. His warning undertone kept them secret and silent till the house was a hundred yards back: then they bolted off into the bush, yelping excitedly. The boy imagined his parents turning in their beds and muttering: Those dogs again!

45. before they were dragged back in sleep; and he smiled scornfully. He always looked back over his shoulder at the house before he passed a wall of trees that shut it from sight. It looked so low and small, crouching there under a

tall and brilliant sky. Then he turned his back on it, and on the frowsting sleepers, and forgot them.

50. He would have to hurry. Before the light grew strong he must be four miles away; and already a tint of green stood in the hollow of a leaf, and the air smelled of morning and the stars were dimming.

He slung the shoes over his shoulder, veld skoen that were crinkled and hard with the dews of a hundred mornings. They would be necessary when the
55. ground became too hot to bear. Now he felt the chilled dust push up between his toes, and he let the muscles of his feet spread and settle into the shapes of the earth; and he thought: I could walk a hundred miles on feet like these! I could walk all day, and never tire!

He was walking swiftly through the dark tunnel of foliage that in daytime
60. was a road. The dogs were invisibly ranging the lower travelways of the bush, and he heard them panting. Sometimes he felt a cold muzzle on his leg before they were off again, scouting for a trail to follow. They were not trained, but free-running companions of the hunt, who often tired of the long stalk before the final shots, and went off on their own pleasure. Soon he could see them,
65. small and wild-looking in a wild strange light, now that the bush stood trembling on the verge of colour, waiting for the sun to paint earth and grass afresh.

The grass stood to his shoulders; and the trees were showering a faint silvery rain. He was soaked; his whole body was clenched in a steady shiver.
70. Once he bent to the road that was newly scored with animal trails, and regretfully straightened, reminding himself that the pleasure of tracking must wait till another day.

He began to run along the edge of a field, noting jerkily how it was filmed over with fresh spiderweb, so that the long reaches of great black clods seemed
75. netted in glistening grey. He was using the steady lope he had learned by watching the natives, the run that is a dropping of the weight of the body from one foot to the next in a slow balancing movement that never tires, nor shortens the breath; and he felt the blood pulsing down his legs and along his arms, and the exultation and pride of body mounted in him till he was shutting
80. his teeth hard against a violent desire to shout his triumph.

Soon he had left the cultivated part of the farm. Behind him the bush was low and black. In front was a long vlei, acres of long pale grass that sent back a hollowing gleam of light to a satiny sky. Near him thick swathes of grass were bent with the weight of water, and diamond drops sparkled on each
85. frond.

The first bird woke at his feet and at once a flock of them sprang into the air calling shrilly that day had come; and suddenly, behind him, the bush woke into song, and he could hear the guinea-fowl calling far ahead of him. That meant they would now be sailing down from their trees into thick grass, and
90. it was for them he had come: he was too late. But he did not mind. He forgot he had come to shoot. He set his legs wide, and balanced from foot to foot, and swung his gun up and down in both hands horizontally, in a kind of improvised exercise, and let his head sink back till it was pillowed in his neck muscles, and watched how above him small rosy clouds floated in a lake of
95. gold.

Suddenly it all rose in him: it was unbearable. He leapt up into the air, shouting and yelling wild, unrecognizable noises. Then he began to run, not carefully, as he had before, but madly, like a wild thing. He was clean crazy, yelling mad with the joy of living and a superfluity of youth. He rushed down
100. the vlei under a tumult of crimson and gold, while all the birds of the world sang about him. He ran in great leaping strides, and shouted as he ran, feeling

his body rise into the crisp rushing air and fall back surely on to sure feet; and thought briefly, not believing that such a thing could happen to him, that he could break his ankle any moment, in this thick tangled grass. He cleared
105. bushes like a duiker, leaped over rocks; and finally came to dead stop at a place where the ground fell abruptly away below him to the river. It had been a two-mile-long dash through waist-high growth, and he was breathing hoarsely and could no longer sing. But he poised on a rock and looked down at stretches of water that gleamed through stooping trees, and thought
110. suddenly, I am fifteen! Fifteen! The words came new to him; so that he kept repeating them wonderingly, with swelling excitement; and he felt the years of his life with his hands, as if he were counting marbles, each one hard and separate and compact, each one a wonderful shining thing. That was what he was: fifteen years of this rich soil, and this slow-moving water, and air that
115. smelt like a challenge whether it was warm and sultry at noon, or as brisk as cold water, like it was now.

There was nothing he couldn't do, nothing! A vision came to him, as he stood there, like when a child hears the word 'eternity' and tries to understand it, and time takes possession of the mind. He felt his life ahead of him as a
120. great and wonderful thing, something that was his; and he said aloud, with the blood rising to his head: all the great men of the world have been as I am now, and there is nothing I can't become, nothing I can't do; there is no country in the world I cannot make part of myself, if I choose. I contain the world. I can make of it what I want. If I choose, I can change everything that
125. is going to happen: it depends on me, and what I decide now.

The urgency, and the truth and courage of what his voice was saying exulted him so that he began to sing again, at the top of his voice, and the sound went echoing down the river gorge. He stopped for the echo, and sang again: stopped and shouted. That was what he was!—he sang, if he chose; and the
130. world had to answer him.

And for minutes he stood there, shouting and singing and waiting for the lovely eddying sound of the echo; so that his own new strong thoughts came back and washed round his head, as if someone were answering him and encouraging him; till the gorge was full of soft voices clashing back and forth
135. from rock to rock over the river. And then it seemed as if there was a new voice. He listened, puzzled, for it was not his own. Soon he was leaning forward, all his nerves alert, quite still: somewhere close to him there was a noise that was no joyful bird, nor tinkle of falling water, nor ponderous movement of cattle.
140. There it was again. In the deep morning hush that held his future and his past, was a sound of pain, and repeated over and over: it was a kind of shortened scream, as if someone, something, had no breath to scream. He came to himself, looked about him and called for the dogs. They did not appear: they had gone off on their own business and he was alone. Now he
145. was clean sober, all the madness gone. His heart beating fast, because of that frightened screaming, he stepped carefully off the rock and went towards a belt of trees. He was moving cautiously, for not so long ago he had seen a leopard in just this spot.

At the end of the trees he stopped and peered, holding his gun ready; he
150. advanced, looking steadily about him, his eyes narrowed. Then, all at once, in the middle of a step, he faltered, and his face was puzzled. He shook his head impatiently, as if he doubted his own sight.

There, between two trees, against a background of gaunt black rocks, was a figure from a dream, a strange beast that was horned and drunken-legged,
155. but like something he had never even imagined. It seemed to be ragged. It

looked like a small buck that had black ragged tufts of fur standing up irregularly all over it, with patches of raw flesh beneath. . .but the patches of rawness were disappearing under moving black and came again elsewhere: and all the time the creature screamed, in small gasping screams, and leaped

160. drunkenly from side to side, as if it were blind.

Then the boy understood: it *was* a buck. He ran closer, and again stood still, stopped by a new fear. Around him the grass was whispering and alive. He looked wildly about, and then down. The ground was black with ants, great energetic ants that took no notice of him, but hurried and scurried

165. towards the fighting shape, like glistening black water flowing through the grass.

And, as he drew in his breath and pity and terror seized him, the beast fell and the screaming stopped. Now he could hear nothing but one bird singing, and the sound of the rustling, whispering ants.

170. He peered over at the writhing blackness that jerked convulsively with the jerking nerves. It grew quieter. There were small twitches from the mass that still looked vaguely like the shape of a small animal.

It came into his mind that he should shoot it and end its pain; and he raised the gun. Then he lowered it again. The buck could no longer feel; its fighting

175. was a mechanical protest of the nerves. But it was not that which made him put down the gun. It was a swelling feeling of rage and misery and protest that expressed itself in the thought: if I had not come it would have died like this: so why should I interfere? All over the bush things like this happen; they happen all the time; this is how life goes on, by living things dying in anguish.

180. He gripped the gun between his knees and felt in his own limbs the myriad swarming pain of the twitching animal that could no longer feel, and set his teeth, and said over and over again under his breath: I can't stop it. I can't stop it. There is nothing I can do.

He was glad that the buck was unconscious and had gone past suffering so

185. that he did not have to make a decision to kill it even when he was feeling with his whole body: this is what happens, this is how things work.

It was right—that was what he was feeling. *It was right and nothing could alter it.*

The knowledge of fatality, of what has to be, had gripped him and for the

190. first time in his life; and he was left unable to make any movement of brain or body, except to say: 'Yes, yes. That is what living is.' It had entered his flesh and his bones and grown into the farthest corners of his brain and would never leave him. And at the moment he could not have performed the smallest action of mercy, knowing as he did, having lived on it all his life, the vast

195. unalterable, cruel veld, where at any moment one might stumble over a skull or crush the skeleton of some small creature.

Suffering, sick, and angry, but also grimly satisfied with his new stoicism, he stood there leaning on his rifle, and watched the seething black mound grow smaller. At his feet, now, were ants trickling back with pink fragments

200. in their mouths, and there was a fresh acid smell in his nostrils. He sternly controlled the uselessly convulsing muscles of his empty stomach, and reminded himself: the ants must eat too! At the same time he found that the tears were streaming down his face, and his clothes were soaked with the sweat of that other creature's pain.

205. The shape had grown small. Now it looked like nothing recognizable. He did not know how long it was before he saw the blackness thin, and bits of white showed through, shining in the sun—yes, there was the sun, just up, glowing over the rocks. Why, the whole thing could not have taken longer than a few minutes.

210.   He began to swear, as if the shortness of the time was in itself unbearable, using the words he had heard his father say. He strode forward, crushing ants with each step and brushing them off his clothes, till he stood above the skeleton, which lay sprawled under a small bush. It was clean-picked. It might have been lying there years, save that on the white bone were pink fragments

215. of gristle. About the bones ants were ebbing away, their pincers full of meat.

    The boy looked at them, big black ugly insects. A few were standing and gazing up at him with small glittering eyes.

    'Go away!' he said to the ants, very coldly. 'I am not for you—not just yet, at any rate. Go away.' And he fancied that the ants turned and went away.

220.   He bent over the bones and touched the sockets in the skull; that was where the eyes were, he thought incredulously, remembering the liquid dark eyes of a buck. And then he bent the slim foreleg bone, swinging it horizontally in his palm.

    That morning, perhaps an hour ago, this small creature had been stepping

225. proud and free through the bush, feeling the chill on its hide even as he himself had done, exhilarated by it. Proudly stepping the earth, tossing its horns, frisking a pretty white tail, it had sniffed the cold morning air. Walking like kings and conquerors it had moved through this free-held bush, where each blade of grass grew for it alone, and where the river ran pure sparkling water

230. for its slaking.

    And then—what had happened? Such a swift surefooted thing could surely not be trapped by a swarm of ants?

    The boy bent curiously to the skeleton. Then he saw that the back leg that lay uppermost and strained out in the tension of death, was snapped midway

235. in the thigh, so that broken bones jutted over each other uselessly. So that was it! Limping into the ant-masses it could not escape, once it had sensed the danger. Yes, but how had the leg been broken? Had it fallen, perhaps? Impossible, a buck was too light and graceful. Had some jealous rival horned it?

240.   What could possibly have happened? Perhaps some Africans had thrown stones at it, as they do, trying to kill it for meat, and had broken its leg. Yes, that must be it.

    Even as he imagined the crowd of running, shouting natives, and the flying stones, and the leaping buck, another picture came into his mind. He saw

245. himself, on any one of these bright ringing mornings, drunk with excitement, taking a snap shot at some half-seen buck. He saw himself with the gun lowered, wondering whether he had missed or not; and thinking at last that it was late, and he wanted his breakfast, and it was not worth while to track miles after an animal that would very likely get away from him in any case.

250.   For a moment he would not face it. He was a small boy again, kicking sulkily at the skeleton, hanging his head, refusing to accept responsibility.

    Then he straightened up, and looked down at the bones with an odd expression of dismay, all the anger gone out of him. His mind went quite empty: all around him he could see trickles of ants disappearing into the grass.

255. The whispering noise was faint and dry, like the rustling of a cast snakeskin.

    At last he picked up his gun and walked homewards. He was telling himself half defiantly that he wanted his breakfast. He was telling himself that it was getting very hot, much too hot to be out roaming the bush.

    Really, he was tired. He walked heavily, not looking where he put his feet.

260. When he came within sight of his home he stopped, knitting his brows. There was something he had to think out. The death of that small animal was a thing that concerned him, and he was by no means finished with it. It lay at the back of his mind uncomfortably.

Soon, the very next morning, he would get clear of everybody and go to
265. the bush and think about it.

A Sunrise on the Veld by **Doris Lessing**

1. From the first *three* paragraphs, what do we learn about the boy Doris Lessing is writing about?
('Every night .... commanded and refused') (6)

2. Explain why you think 'he smiled scornfully'? Line 45. (3)

3. 'Suddenly it all rose in him: it was unbearable.' Line 96.
Explain what you think this means. (4)

4. What methods does the author use to make us share the boy's joy of living and his feelings of power? (6)

5. (a) His mood suddenly changes. Why? (5)

   (b) What new emotions and thoughts does he experience with this change of mood? (6)

6. What do you think this paragraph means? 'For a moment he would not face it .... the responsibility.' Lines 250 and 251. (4)

7. What do you think the boy learns from his outing that morning? (6)

40 Marks

Paper 2, Comprehension B

Read the following articles and then answer the questions.

A. **Flight Path to a Good Tip** (*The Guardian,* 22.3.84)

Gulls head for Sweden or Switzerland for the spring. In winter they come back to Surrey —and rubbish. Stephen Young reports.

1 Birds and aeroplanes populate the same habitat. As a result, they occasionally collide, sometimes with tragic and expensive consequences. But the risk of bird strikes could be reduced if we could persuade feathered aviators to avoid the flight lanes used by their human counterparts. That was the rationale behind a recent inquiry into the ecology of seagulls, conducted by scientists at the Ministry of Agriculture, Fisheries and Food (MAFF).

2 Two reasons lay behind the scientists' decision to study seagulls. Firstly, over 40 per cent of all collisions between birds and aircraft in Britain involve gulls. Secondly, the population of Britain's seagulls is still on the increase. According to the British Trust for Ornithology, well over a million seagulls now spend winter inland in Britain, com-pared with only 333,000 30 years ago.

3 The scientists, N. Horton, T. Brough and J.B.A. Rochard, concentrated their attention on gulls that forage on refuse tips to the south west of London and roost on the Thames Valley reservoirs— near Heathrow Airport. The majority of these birds are black-headed gulls, but the great and lesser black-backed gulls, as well as common and herring gulls, are also frequent visitors to the area.

4 The number of gulls in this population reaches a peak in mid-winter, then declines rapidly as the birds leave the home counties for a variety of more exotic destinations. Some gulls repair to parts of southern Britain, but the majority disperse to breeding grounds on the Continent.

5 Gulls ringed by the scientists from MAFF have turned up at a remarkably wide range of sites in continental Europe, from Sweden to Switzerland and from Finland to Poland. Among these European resorts, Denmark and the Netherlands are the most popular with London's gulls.

6 At the close of the breeding season, many birds will return to scavenge on Surrey's rubbish. Some will even return to feed at tips they frequented during the preceding winter. This attachment to a particular feeding site seems to endure from year to year. The scientists found that birds ringed at a given tip were much more likely to return there in later years than would have been expected by chance.

7 Gulls are clearly creatures of habit. On their daily journeys between roost and refuse, they keep to distinct, widely used flight paths, which seem to follow natural landmarks, such as river valleys. This regular beha-viour persists even when gulls have been forced by pressure of events to find a new tip. In such circumstances, they tend to continue foraging in the same area and to adhere to former flight lines.

8 Rubbish tips offer gulls a highly attractive supply of rich pickings. Consequently, they will fly up to 30 miles from their watery roosts to visit a favourite site. In these man-made larders, the abundance of food, and its density,

enable the birds to satisfy their daily needs in a relatively short time. So it comes as no sur-prise to learn that seagulls spend hours each day loafing near the tips. This concerns the scientists, not because they object to sloth in seagulls, but because they infer that the sources of refuse available to our wintering gulls are only partially exploited at present.

9 Similarly, the birds' roosts on reservoirs appear capable of supporting greater numbers than currently use them.

10 If our population of sea-gulls does continue to expand, the need to plan rubbish dis-posal with reference to the birds' ecology will become more pressing. A rubbish tip —which, from a gull's eye view, must seem like an enor-mous bird-table—is a major attraction for seagulls. What's more, it brings large numbers of birds into a wide surround-ing area. And a tip doesn't have to be near a roost in order to be a target for the region's gulls; they are willing to travel. If their commuting habits are not to clash with ours, we have to locate new tips with great care.

Reference: N. Horton, T. Brough, J.B.A. Rochard, Journal of Applied Ecology, vol. 20, p751, 1983.

B. **Lapwing Feathers a Nest on Jet Runway**
(*Lancashire Evening Post,* 1.6.84)

Pictures:
Michael Edwards

IS IT A BIRD, IS IT A PLANE. . .OR BOTH?

Mr Murphy

1 This daring bird has nested in the middle of a runway used by giant Canberra jet bombers.

2 But officials at the British Aerospace airfield at Samlesbury, near Preston, are in no hurry to evict the lapwing, for it has become a firm favourite with the workers.

3 Nature-spotters are baffled by the lapwing which has laid her eggs on Runway 18—right in the path of the bombers.

4 Two oystercatchers are also living dangerously nearby on the edge of the runway—and don't turn so much as a feather when the planes zoom past.

5 Bird-watcher Mr Bill Murphy, who discovered the nest, said: 'This is the most amazing nest site that I have seen. Perhaps they feel safe because the airfield is completely fenced.'

6 Oystercatchers nest more traditionally on the shoreline or in shingle river banks. Loose stones on the edge of the runway are now home for their spotted eggs.

7 'They are very amusing birds—especially when returning to the nest and look quite funny pottering across the tarmac on bright pink legs.' added Mr Murphy of Daisy Meadow, Clayton Brook, near Chorley.

8 So far the birds have not been any trouble. Aircraft Supt Mr Len Asher said: 'Birds on runways can be a nuisance, even dangerous, but the oystercatchers seem very obliging. They have certainly created a lot of interest and many employees watch them at lunch-time.'

Article A

1. What do you understand by the term 'bird strikes' in paragraph one? (2)

2. According to paragraph two, why did the scientists at the Ministry of Agriculture, Fisheries and Food decide to study seagulls? (2)

3. Read paragraphs three to ten which describe the findings of the research undertaken by the three scientists Horton, Brough and Rochard. *Make notes* on the types of gulls studied, their destinations during the breeding season, their feeding habits in Surrey and the conclusions the scientists reached. (10)

4. In the article as a whole, gulls are compared to humans several times. Quote *two* examples and then comment on the effectiveness of the two comparisons. (6)

Article B

5. In the first sentence of the article, how is the fact that the lapwing has nested on a runway made more significant? (2)

6. What factual information is given about the oystercatchers' nesting habits and what reason is offered for their choosing the airfield? (2)

7. What is the attitude of (a) the officials and (b) the employees at the British Aerospace airfield towards the lapwing and the oystercatchers? (3)

8. What characteristics are accorded to the lapwing and the oystercatchers by the human observers? (4)

Both Articles

9. Look at the headlines and introductory sub-headings of both articles. How effective are they? Explain how they achieve their effect. (5)

10. There are four photographs accompanying these two articles. Taking each one in turn, say what you think it contributes to the effectiveness of the article as a whole. (4)

40 Marks

PAPER 1 EXPRESSION

Section A

A1 Strikes

A2 The First World War

A3 Astrology

Section B

Essays

PAPER 2 UNDERSTANDING

Comprehension A:

Brackley and the Bed by Samual Selvon

Comprehension B:

A Hell of a Hotel

Paper 1, Section A

A1. Strikes

*Here are the views of a few people on the subject of strikes. Study them carefully, then write an **essay** saying what **your** views are. You **must** refer to at least **some** of the views expressed here but you may add some of your own.*

Mr White
'Strikes are immoral!'

A Striker's Wife
'It's all right striking for a principle, but principles don't pay the rent or feed the children, do they? My husband has been on strike for weeks now and I just can't manage.'

Union Representative
'Working men have to stick together. They don't have the education or the wealth to make them powerful; their only power lies in their unity. If their union tells them to strike, when every other way has failed, then they must strike.'

Journalist
'Sometimes workers strike out of fear. They are afraid that their particular industry or community might be destroyed, or their jobs might be at stake.'

Businessman
'Most workers don't want to strike. They want to earn enough money to pay the bills, eat, have a holiday and have a decent standard of living. But they have to do as they are told by their powerful union bosses.'

Retired Worker
'If you look in your history books into the conditions of working class men, you'll see that they've always been exploited. It's no wonder that they band together and come out on strike when they feel that their bosses are misusing them.'

Nurse
'I listen to the news and hear about people in most professions being given decent salary increases. Then I compare it with what I'm usually given. Is it any wonder that I strike? I work hard; I'm on my feet for many hours each day. Why shouldn't I be allowed to have a decent standard of living too?'

A Moderate
'Arbitration is the only answer to industrial problems. Striking should be made illegal.'

Paper 1, Section A

A2. The First World War

*Here are two passages and a poem about the First World War. After reading them carefully, imagine that you were there in the trenches; then write a **talk for radio** describing your experiences. You may add any material of your own.*

Dulce et Decorum est by Wilfred Owen

Bent double, like old beggars under sacks,
Knock-kneed, coughing like hags, we cursed through sludge,
Till on the haunting flares we turned our backs,
And towards our distant rest began to trudge.
Men marched asleep. Many had lost their boots
But limped on, blood-shod. All went lame; all blind;
Drunk with fatigue; deaf even to the hoots
Of gas-shells dropping softly behind.

Gas! GAS! Quick, boys! — an ecstasy of fumbling,
Fitting the clumsy helmets just in time;
But someone still was yelling out and stumbling
And flound'ring like a man in fire or lime ...
Dim, through the misty panes and thick green light,
As under a green sea, I saw him drowning.

In all my dreams, before my helpless sight,
He plunges at me, guttering, choking, drowning.
If in some smothering dreams you too could pace
Behind the wagon that we flung him in,
And watch the white eyes writhing in his face,
His hanging face, like a devil's sick of sin;
If you could hear, at every jolt, the blood
Come gargling from the froth-corrupted lungs,
Bitter as the cud
Of vile, incurable sores on innocent tongues, -
My friend, you would not tell with such high zest
To children ardent for some desperate glory,
The old lie: Dulce et decorum est
*Pro patria mori. **

* How sweet and fitting it is to die for one's country

From 'A History of Britain 1900-1939' by John Ray (London, 1967)

People often ask 'What was it like to fight in the trenches in the First World War?' No full answer can be given. Words alone cannot bring an understanding of the fears, the hardships and closeness to death that men knew. For most of the war, on the Western Front, the armies remained like two wrestlers, locked in a terrible combat. They were so evenly matched that neither side could gain a decisive victory.

 The weapons of modern war drove men underground. Powerful artillery fire, quick firing rifles and the murderous machine gun sent the armies to shelter in dug- outs and trenches behind lines of barbed wire.

 The casualty figures were enormous. Every English town and village has its war memorial showing the names of local men who fell in France or Belgium. It is tragic to see that sometimes in a family three or four sons, usually aged between 18 and 35, left their home and never returned.

From 'The Deluge. British Society and the First World War' by Arthur Marwick (London and Basingstoke, 1973)

What people at home heard of the fighting man's war was only a confused murmur. They knew the statistics of death—nearly 20,000 killed on 1st July, the first day of the Battle of the Somme—but not the foul horror of it; they saw the glory, but not the sordid filth of trench life. Fighting men, appalled at the nature of the war in which they found themselves, were unable to convey the unbelievable substance.

'There are some things better left undescribed . . . Perhaps in the afterwards when time has deadened matters, you will hear of them,' wrote one young soldier.

Paper 1, Section A

A3. Astrology

*Referring to **some** of the facts and opinions contained in each of (a), (b) and (c), write EITHER the case for OR the case against astrology.*

You may, if you wish, use additional information of your own.

(a) 'Star Wallahs in The Ascendency' (*The Times*, 13 January, 1983)

Star wallahs in the ascendancy

Delhi
An Indan newspaper with its feet firmly planted in the hardheaded business community, the *Economic Times,* recently carried two pages devoted to astrology, complete with a national horoscope and forecasts of shares, harvests, oil finds and interest rates.

None of this was tongue-in-cheek: in India little of importance happens without the involvement of astrologers, and many businessmen consult their prophets as well as their bankers.

According to the newspaper's star wallahs, planetary influences will ensure good harvests and buoyant share markets, help to contain inflation and make India self-sufficient in oil.

The importance of astrology to life in India shows no sign of diminishing. Events large and small are arranged in consultation with compilers of horoscopes. Bridges, dams and buildings are started on auspicious days, as is ploughing and planting.

Marriages are usually arranged after couples have had their horoscopes checked for compatibility, and there are particular times of the year decreed as especially auspicious for weddings, when the streets are jammed with marriage processions and filled with the raucous din of wedding bands.

Parents make a point of recording the exact time of a baby's birth so that an accurate horoscope can be cast. People carry this through their lives, rather like a health record, producing it for expert perusal at emotional and professional crossroads.

Business executives often consult palmists and seers before embarking on deals or business journeys. Bank managers sometimes take customers wanting a loan to an astrologer to see if there is any malign planetary force that might prevent repayment.

Some businessmen contemplating a partnership take their prospective colleagues' photographs and birth date to an astrologer for assessment. This practice, according to one of the astrologers in the *Economic Times*, is being adopted by American and European firms in an effort to make employers and new employees compatible.

There are said to be 300,000 astrologers in India, ranging from men in ragged *dhotis* who work on city pavements and offer a consultation for a few rupees, to sleekly prosperous men in smart offices charging high fees.

In Bombay, India's commercial and film capital, 75,000 astrologers are playing their part in big-money decisions. More than 150 astrological magazines are published throughout the country.

It is widely believed in India that politicians are the most regular attenders at astrologers' offices and that election dates and other important matters are often decided after consultation with fortune-tellers.

"Belief in astrology, palmistry and numerology is very strong among us Indians", the *Hindustan Times* lamented recently. "Fortune-telling has developed into a lucrative art for which the gullible fall. It is a paradox that in a scientific age astrology engages the attention of millions of civilized people."

Astrologers who have just attended a conference in Delhi called for greater official recognition of their trade. They want astrology taught in schools, and point out that only one university offers a degree course in the subject.

It was rather unfortunate that so soon after demanding to be taken more seriously, the astrologers did not shine in their first big test of the year. Hardly any fortune-teller seems to have done well in the recent elections in which Mrs Indira Gandhi, the Prime Minister, suffered traumatic defeats.

Not long before the elections one of the astrologers writing in the *Economic Times* said that the position of the Sun and Mars gave Mrs Gandhi unequalled power and that she was in complete control of Indian affairs.

One, however, said he feared a bad patch in the Prime Minister's life, with a critical period between March and June. But another said that Mrs Gandhi's vibrations were good, yet another that the elections would raise her prestige and enable her to conquer her enemies. Oh well, back to the star charts.

Trevor Fishlock

(b) Stars Shine in Your Eyes. (*The Listener*, 24 February, 1983)

If the BBC started reporting regularly on the activities of elves and fairies, employed weathermen who used chunks of seaweed and consulted their corns, and devoted screen-time to serious discussion of the latest perpetual motion machine, we might be justified in thinking that all rational beings had fled from its higher management and left Television Centre to the simple-minded.

The inclusion of astrologers in both breakfast television programmes is scarcely less disturbing, for astrology appears to have been accepted as a perfectly normal component of the business of starting the day, on a par with traffic news, meteorology, the state of the pound and gardening hints. The trouble is, all the other necessary parts of daily life owe something to the normal processes of human reasoning. We would be entitled to complain if our traffic information came from a member of a group of people whose predictions of traffic hold-ups in the past had usually totally disagreed with one another and with reality, and who had given us such useful forecasts as: There could quite possibly be traffic delays for some of you today, particularly those with X registered cars, on some roads approaching some cities in Britain.

There are two possible explanations for why people in television, and indeed the world at large, may put up with astrology. The first could be that they don't really take astrology seriously, but feel that, as a source of totally unbelievable fun, it is harmless and attracts an audience who see it in a similarly light-hearted way—what does it matter if, in the end, it turns out to be a good year for cancer, instead of a good year for Cancer. Unfortunately, I believe that the attitude of many of the audience who listen to the words of wisdom from the breakfast astrologer is far from light-hearted. Many people are predisposed to believe in the irrational as a release from the world of unemployment, personal failure, unhappy relationships and sickness.

The BBC astrologer, for example, said recently: 'Today is good for work prospects for Cancerians, so it's a good time, especially if you're unemployed, to go out and get that job that you've always wanted.' This piece of nonsense may well have given a few people hope for the day, until they found that the stars had actually made no difference to job prospects.

The second explanation for why some people are charitably disposed towards astrology could be that they don't know enough about it to dismiss it and probably think there might even be something in it. But those astrological statements that are not so vague as to be meaningless can actually be tested, to see whether there is any validity at all in the suggested linkages between the characteristics of individuals and their signs of the zodiac.

Indeed, it has actually been done. Michel and Francoise Gauquelin have spent the past 20 years examining most of the more fashionable astrological theories for evidence of correlations between personality characteristics and signs of the zodiac. They have used birth data on more than 40,000 people in Europe and have tried to find links between birth signs, occupation and personality traits. Their results were awaited with interest, partly because these were not sceptics attempting to disprove astrology, but people who wanted to believe that there was 'something in it'. Computerised number-crunching of a high order was used to make sure that no potential correlation was untested. Their conclusions could not be more clear-cut. There was nothing in it. 'Every attempt, whether of astrologers or scientists, to produce evidence of astrological laws has been in vain. It is now quite certain that the signs in the sky which preside over our births have no power whatever to decide our fates, to affect our heredity or characteristics, or to play any part, however humble, in the totality of effects, random and otherwise, which form the fabric of our lives and mould our impulses to action.'

It's easy to dismiss an attack on astrology or the paranormal as overreacting to a bit of harmless fun. But I don't think anything is harmless which persuades people that there are soft options in thinking, reasoning and understanding the world. Why bother with physics if metal can be bent with thought waves? Why bother with medicine, psychology or the social sciences if random arrangements of stars and planets can heal you or improve your personal relationships? In the end, astrology is founded on self-deceit or deceit of others, and I don't think that either the BBC or the IBA should be colluding in this.

Karl Sabbagh

(c) Do the Stars Shape Our Destinies After All?

In early 1984, Professor Alan Smithers of Manchester University completed a survey of 2.3 million people to investigate the relationship of people's jobs and the sign under which they were born.

Here is an extract from his introductory article on the subject. There follows some statistical evidence to support the survey's findings.

(*The Guardian*, 19 March, 1984)

With the help of the Koestler Foundation and The Guardian, it has been possible to purchase from the Office of Population Censuses and Surveys a special tabulation of information collected in the 1971 Census, the latest one for which the data we wanted are currently available.

The office was able to provide a one in ten sample of all 'economically active persons,' which includes those in employment, those who were sick at the time of the census, and those available for work but who did not have a job. Only those born in Britain and usually resident here were included. The sample was massive, comprising 1,461,874 men and 842,799 women, each assigned to one of 223 occupational groups. Occupation and date of birth has never before been studied so systematically.

The year was divided into twelve nearly equal periods beginning at the usual date for the spring equinox, March 21—appropriately enough Wednesday—which is the starting point for both the

127

astrological and seasonal years. The periods were chosen to correspond to the twelve zodiac signs and they are also equivalent to the traditional dates for spring, summer, autumn, and winter, each divided into three. So the basic data were two (sex) 12 (birth period) x 223 (occupations) tables.

Unlike the studies based on reference books, the birth curve for the adult working population was no problem. It was obtained simply from the totals for each birth period. Interestingly, as we shall be seeing tomorrow, almost identical curves were obtained for men and women, with in each case a peak in April/May and a trough in October/November. The difference between maximum and minimum frequencies of birth was about 13 per cent.

When the birth distributions for the individual occupations were compared to the general curve, some showed what seemed to be seasonal trends with several successive periods either above or below average. People in the professions and show business, it seems, are born in the spring, typists in the summer, clerks and miners in the autumn, and electricians and car mechanics in the winter.

The seasonality becomes even more apparent if larger groupings such as the social classes are considered. As we will be seeing tomorrow, there is clear evidence that those in the better jobs tend to be born in the spring.

But other occupations varied in less obvious ways and the question arises: could this conceivably have anything to do with astrology? It is a time-honoured tradition in astrology that a person's character and destiny are in some way linked with the time of birth. Although for a serious astrologer dividing the year into 12 sun signs is a gross over-simplification of a complex and subtle art, in their popular writings astrologers often do include advice on occupations. But for the uninitiated it is not easy to make sense of the wide variety of suggestions that are offered. Teach Yourself Astrology, for example, lists for Pisces, the sign which the sun is just leaving, musician, artist, lyrical writer, poet, actor, priest, sailor, social worker—and chiropodist!

In some confusion, I turned to Charles Harvey, president of the Astrological Association, who helped me to organise a survey of the opinions of some of the most expert and well-qualified astrologers in the country. He also, in explaining the principles on which astrologers operate, made several predic-

tions. This was without any knowledge of the results.

One of Charles Harvey's suggestions was that people in the caring professions, and here he specifically mentioned nursing, could be expected, other things being equal, to be more frequently in alternate signs beginning with Taurus, which to an astrologer are the feminine or supportive signs. Conversely, for alternate signs from Aries, which are the assertive or masculine signs, he predicted that above average numbers of trade union officials would be born.

Incredibly, as you can see from the graphs, these predictions turned out to be correct. Although the alternation is not perfect, the patterns are striking and statistically significant. Why there should be this switching from sign to sign is hard to see.

An astrologer would explain it by saying that personality is related to time of birth and that where, as in nursing and running a trade union, personality can be expressed through occupation, such a result is to be expected. However, for sceptics like myself, it is difficult to accept that personality is modulated in this way.

It is true that when personality has been studied directly a sawtooth pattern for extroversion has sometimes been

found, with the more extrovert and the more introvert being found in alternate signs from Aries onwards. But this is usually thought to reflect the way personality has been measured which usually depends on people describing themselves. In filling in a self-report inventory people will draw on the hints and clues available to them and some of these may have come from all the allusions to astrology in the media and elsewhere.

If you hear often enough that your star sign says you are outgoing and impulsive, you may bring it into your answers when faced with a personality questionnaire. The serious business of getting a job though is something else.

Not all Charles Harvey's predictions were correct. He suggested that salesmen, who he assumed to be extrovert, would be born mainly in alternate signs from Aries and this proved not to be the case. Nevertheless, since he had got it right on two occasions it seemed worth looking for other possible astrological associations and some were found.

The study has turned up a mass of extraordinary data. Much of it cannot be explained. But because we are dealing with a large representative sample of the whole population, we can have confidence in the findings.

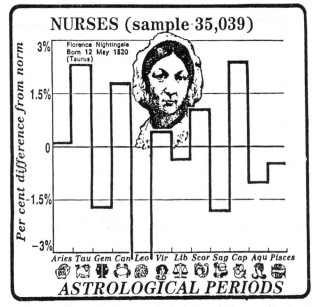

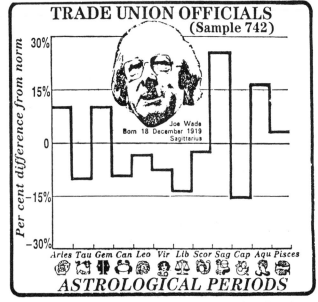

The president of the Astrological Association predicted that nurses might frequently be born under Taurus and trade union officials under Sagittarius. Incredibly, he was right.

Paper 1, Section B

Write about two sides on ONE of the following. Your aim should be to produce an imaginative and lively piece of writing.

B1. The Collier's Wife

*The collier's wife had four tall sons
Brought from the pit's mouth dead,
And crushed from foot to head;
When others brought her husband home,
Had five dead bodies in her room.*

*Had five dead bodies in her house -
All in a row they lay -
To bury in one day.
Such sorrow in the valley has
Made kindness grow like grass.*

*Oh collier, collier, underground,
In fear of fire and gas,
What life more danger has?
Who fears more danger in this life?
There is but one—thy wife!*

W.H. Davies

This poem highlights the grave dangers involved in coal mining and the suffering the miners' wives must endure. Write a story about any job you consider dangerous from *the point of view of a close relative* of the person doing the job.

B2. The Duel.

B3. Describe your experiences going from door to door, whilst delivering milk or delivering newspapers, or asking for sponsorship or canvassing for a local political candidate.

B4. 'Life begins at forty.' Describe someone you know to whom this saying applies.

B5. You have just received the name and address of a new pen friend who lives abroad. Write your first letter to him or her.

B6. The conspiracy.

B7. At your parents' silver wedding anniversary you have to make a speech paying tribute to them. Write your speech.

B8. 'You let me down!'
Describe an occasion when this was said to you OR when you said this to someone else.

B9. Nightmare.

B10. Study the photograph and write about it in any way you choose.

Paper 2, Comprehension A

Read the short story below and then answer the questions which follow.

Brackley And The Bed by **Samuel Selvon**, from 'Ways of Sunlight'
(Davis-Poynter)

One evening Brackley was cruising round by the Embankment looking for a
soft bench to rest his weary bones, and to cogitate on the ways of life. The
reason for that, and the reason why the boys begin to call him Rockabye, you
will find out as the ballad goes on.

5. Brackley hail from Tobago, which part they have it to say Robinson Crusoe
used to hang out with Man Friday. Things was brown in that island and he
make for England and manage to get a work and was just settling down when
bam! he get a letter from his aunt saying that Teena want to come England
too.

10. Teena was Brackley distant cousin and they was good friends in Tobago.
In fact, the other reason why Brackley hustle from the island is because it did
look like he and Teena was heading for a little married thing, and Brackley
run.

Well, right away he write aunty and say no, no, because he have a feeling
15. this girl would make botheration if she come England. The aunt write back
to say she didn't mean to say that Teena want to come England, but that Teena
left Tobago for England already.

Brackley hold his head and bawl. And the evening the boat train come in
at Waterloo, he went there and start 'busing she right away not waiting to ask
20. how the folks at home was or anything.

'What you doing in London?' Brackley ask as soon as Teena step off the
train. 'What you come here for, eh? Even though I write home to say things
real hard?'

'What happen, you buy the country already?' Teena sheself giving tit for
25. tat right away. 'You ruling England now? The Queen abdicate?'

'You know where you going?' Brackley say. 'You know where you is? You
know what you going to do?'

'I am going straight to the Colonial Office,' Teena say.

'What you think the Colonial Office is, eh? You think they will do anything
30. for you? You have a god-father working there?'

Well, they argue until in the end Brackley find himself holding on to Teena
suitcase and they on the way to the little batchy he have in Golders Green at
the time.

When they get there Teena take one look at the room and sniff. 'But look
35. at the state you have this room in! You ain't ashamed of yourself?'

'Listen,' Brackley say, 'you better don't let me and you have contention.
I know this would of happen when you come.'

Teena start squaring up the room brisk-brisk.

'It making cold,' she say, putting chair this way and table that way and
40. turning everything upside down for poor Brackley. 'How you does keep
warm? Where the gas fire I hear so much about?'

Brackley grudgingly put a shilling in the meter and light the gas.

'What you have to eat?' But even as she asking she gone in the cupboard
and begin pulling out rations that Brackley had stow away to see him through
45. the winter. Brackley as if he mesmerise, stand up there watching her as she
start up a peas and rice on the gas ring.

'You better go easy with them rations,' he say. 'I not working now and money don't grow on tree here as in Tobago.'

When they was eating Teena say: 'Well you have to get a job right away.
50. You was always a lazy fellar.'

'Keep quiet,' Brackley say, enjoying the meal that Teena cook in real West Indian fashion—the first good meal he ever had in London. 'You don't know nothing.'

'First thing tomorrow morning,' Teena say. 'What time you get up?'
55. 'About nine—ten,' Brackley say vaguely.

'Well is six o'clock tomorrow morning, bright and early as the cock crow.'

'You don't hear cock crowing in London,' Brackley say. Then he drop the spoon he was eating with. 'Six o'clock! You must be mad! Six o'clock like midnight in the winter, and people still sound asleep.'
60. 'Six o'clock,' Teena say.

Brackley finish eating and begin to smoke, whistling a calypso softly, as if he in another world and not aware of Teena at all.

'Ah well,' he say, stretching by the fire, 'that wasn't a bad meal. Look, I will give you some old blankets and you could wrap up that coat use as a
65. pillow—you could sleep on the ground in that corner ...'

'**Me**? On the floor? You not ashamed?'

'Well, is only one bed here as you see ...'

'I using the bed.'

'Girl, is winter, and if you think I going to sleep in the corner with two old
70. blanket and wake up stiff ...'

But, in the end, was Brackley who crouch up in the corner, and Teena sound asleep in the bed.

It look to Brackley like he hardly shut his eyes before Teena was shaking him.
75. 'Get up,' Teena say, 'six o'clock.'

Brackley start to curse.

'None of that,' Teena say. 'No bad language when I around.'

Teena move around fast and give Brackley breakfast and make him dress and get out on the cold streets mumbling, 'Get a job, get a job,' before he
80. knew what happening.

It was only about ten o'clock, when he was washing dishes in a cafe where he get a work, that Brackley realize what was happening to him.

When he get home in the evening, Teena have screen put up around the bed and everything spick and span, and Brackley don't know where to look even
85. for chair to sit down.

'I see you make yourself at home,' he say maliciously.

'And what you think?' Teena flares.

'The boys does come here sometimes for a little rummy.'

'None of that now.'
90. 'So you taking over completely.'

'Aunty say to look after you.'

'Why the hell you come England, eh?'

Well, a pattern begin to form as the weeks go by, but the main thing that have Brackley worried is the bed. Every night he curl up in the corner
95. shivering, and by the time he doze off: 'Six o'clock, get up, you have to go to work.'

Brackley ain't sleep on bed for weeks. The thing like an obsession with him. He window-shopping on the way home and looking at them bed and soft mattress on show and closing his eyes and sighing. Single divan, double divan,
100. put-you-up, put-you-down—all makes and sizes he looking at.

One night when frost was forming on the window pane Brackley wake up and find he couldn't move.

'Teena.'

'What?'

105. 'You sleeping?'

'Yes.'

'Teena, you want to get married?'

'Married? To who?'

'To me.'

110. 'What for?'

'So-I-could-sleep-in-the-bed—I mean, well, we uses to know one another good in Tobago, and now that you here in London, what you think?'

'Well, all right, but you have to change your ways.'

'Yes, Teena.'

115. 'And no foolishness when we married. You come home straight from work. And I don't want you looking at no white girls.'

'Yes, Teena.'

No sooner said than done. Brackley hustle Teena off to the registry office as soon as things was fixed, thinking only how nice the bed would be after

120. the hard floor and the cold, with Teena to help keep him warm.

'What about honeymoon?' Teena say after the ceremony.

'In the summer,' Brackley say. 'Let we go home. I am tired and I feel I could sleep for weeks.'

'Bracks,' Teena say as they was coming away, 'I have a nice surprise for

125. you. Guess who coming to London this evening?'

'Father Christmas,' Brackley says yawning.

'No, Aunty. I write telling her to come up, as the room not so small and we could manage until we get another place. And then she and me could get a work too, and that will help.'

130. 'You putting hell 'pon jackass back,' Brackley moan. But it was only when they reach home that a great fear come to Brackley. He had was to sit down in a chair before he could talk.

'But Teena,' he say quietly, 'we ain't have no place for Aunty to sleep.'

'Don't worry,' Teena say, 'She can sleep with me until we find another

135. place.'

Brackley and the Bed by **Samuel Selvon**

1. What do you learn about Brackley from the first two paragraphs?   (4)

2. Why did Brackley 'hold his head and bawl'? Line 18.   (4)

3. What is the effect of using so many questions between lines 18 and 33 ('Brackley hold his head and bawl ....in Golders Green at the time')? (4)

4. In a paragraph describe how Brackley's life is changed by Teena.   (10)

5. Why does the author say of the bed, 'The thing like an obsession with him'? Line 97.   (4)

6. How does the language of this story help to make it more effective?   (5)

7. What does Brackley mean when he says to Teena, 'You putting hell 'pon jackass back'? Line 130.   (4)

8. Comment on the humour in this story.   (5)

40 Marks

Paper 2, Comprehension B

Answer the questions on the newspaper article printed below.

A Hell Of A Hotel (Guardian Women, Monday, 5 March 1984)

The bed-and-breakfast hotel is the modern equivalent of the old workhouse. It serves the same purpose and is punitive in intent. It tests the genuine desperation of families awaiting rehousing.

1 THE HOTEL looked seedy, but respectable, from the outside. The plate glass doors bore stickers welcoming Diners Club, Mastercharge and American Express. Just inside the door was a rack filled with brochures for the National Theatre, the Royal Opera House, and West End shows. But this hotel's residents were unlikely to be paying by credit card for a night at the opera. The only 'Dining' available to the Diners Club card holder was a regulatory roll and cold coffee in a dank basement room at breakfast.

2 This is one of the notorious bed-and-breakfast hotels where the homeless are crowded together in squalid misery, dumped by local authorities with nowhere else to put them. The occasional bemused tourist does stay here too, usually by accident, not design. The brochures and credit card signs keep up the shabby pretence that this, and 50 similar others in London's crowded Bayswater, are still hotels. In fact they are tenement slums, many of them plagued by rats, mice, lice, bed-bugs and constant outbreaks of gastro-enteritis in the children.

3 Other cities have their own such hotels to house their growing numbers of homeless—now officially put at 73,600 households (not individuals), but estimated by experts to stand at three times that figure, rising sharply year by year.

4 The hotels have grandiose names. This one housed 500 homeless people, most of them families with children. The old stain-sodden carpet gave off a sour smell. The bannisters were broken in places, leaving lethal gaping drops for small children. The partitioning of rooms made the place a warren of corridors and cramped winding staircases—a death trap from which few residents could hope to escape in a fire. The bathrooms were squalid and shared by five or more families. There were no cooking facilities at all—though most families had an illegal electric ring in their room, another perpetual danger to their children.

5 Each room had just space for the beds and a sink—a double bed and two bunks in the first one I entered, but not enough room for the whole family to stand up at once. They had nowhere to keep food, but a small cupboard which also held the few clothes and possessions they had room for. Some of the hotels have a cooker in the basement six floors down for the use of scores of families—no fridges or laundries. Washing has to be dried on the radiator in the room.

6 I was asked not to mention the names of the hotels I visited. The residents feel too vulnerable, both to their local authorities who placed them there, and the shark-like hotel proprietors, to dare risk being accused of having brought in a visitor, let alone a journalist. Who owns these hotels, none of the residents had been able to ascertain, but several were part of a highly profitable group. Since each family was being charged more than £120 a week for their tiny, sordid box rooms, the landlords' profits must be colossal. (One woman returning to the hotel from hospital with her three-day-old baby was charged an extra £35 for having the child in her room.)

7 Down the winding passages, each narrow hotel room gives onto a scene of human misery and despair. A woman, her husband, and three children under the age of six were crammed into one room with a rough con-

structed sleeping platform taking up the top of the high ceilinged space. They had been living in a caravan before, and had now been in the hotel only a couple of months. But they had a five month stretch in the place before, when they were driven to such despair that they left to camp out again—a serious error. Now they had to begin the waiting all over again, and that five months had all been for nothing.

8 One woman had just come out of hospital with a new tiny baby. There was not enough room for her to put up the cot stacked in one corner and the baby slept curled up on the bed. The curtains were shut, and she scarcely went out, having no pram. She was told she had to go to register the child, collect his National Health card, register with a doctor, take the baby to the clinic, go down to the DHSS and apply for a grant for a pram. She didn't know this part of London, seemed vague, depressed, alone, uprooted, and utterly unable to cope.

9 These people have no social workers to help them through the complex bureaucracy of poverty. They belong to the distant authorities who have dumped them here, and not to Westminster where the hotels are. Westminster do not regard them as their responsibility, so they appoint no social worker to help them.

10 How did they come to be so utterly homeless that one tiny room was the only alternative to the streets? Sheila is a nurse and her husband a plasterer. They have two small boys, of two and three. They have been living in the hotel now for 19 long months, waiting and hoping for the chance of a flat. When they first married they lived with

friends, but then they had a baby and Sheila became accidentally pregnant again soon afterwards. 'We couldn't stay. They told us to go. We had a row in the end when the council tried to get them to take us back. So the council sent us here—for a few weeks they said. Now it's been 19 months.'

11 She is a woman of great energy and resource, determined that her children should not suffer. She has seen plenty of women fall into lethargy and deep depression in their hotel rooms. So she takes her children out all day every day, to the library, swimming, round the shops and to a playgroup. 'I keep them awake all day so they'll sleep as soon as we get back to the room. Sundays are worst, with my husband home, and everything shut, nowhere to go, all of us in the room. We try to sleep as much as we can.'

12 Sandra also keeps out all day with her two children. Her husband works and they have been in the hotel for 16 months. They were evicted from their one-bedroom private flat, though they fought it through the courts. Her oldest boy was in his first year at school, and she didn't want to move him away. 'The council said we'd be here a few weeks, and the school left his place open. That was 16 months ago. It's impossible to get him into a school here. There are no places.' She describes what it was like arriving at the hotel. 'I couldn't believe it, such a small space for all of us, nowhere to cook. I wouldn't use a ring, as it's too dangerous with small children. I felt dead, dead inside. I couldn't believe this was happening to us.'

13 In the hotels too, there are

those given temporary housing for being 'vulnerable', usually those released from mental hospital. Sheila and Sandra described drug addicts and deranged people wandering around the corridors, frightening them and their children. 'One battered on the door the other day, shouting and yelling to be let in. I screamed at him to go away, but no-one came.'

14 These, believe it or not, are among the lucky homeless. They have, at least, been taken on by their local authorities. They are on the waiting lists for a flat, their authority has shouldered responsibility for them. These are among the 73,600 that appear in the official figures. Most experts estimate the actual number to be three times that figure—a fact not disputed by a Government spokesman in the House of Lords recently. The Homeless Persons Act allows authorities to turn away those deemed to have made themselves 'intentionally homeless', and some authorities use this loophole ruthlessly. All the families I spoke to had been grilled about this and some of them were indignant: 'Would you put yourself here if you had anywhere else to go?' one said fiercely.

15 The bed-and-breakfast hotel is the modern equivalent of the old workhouse. It serves the same purpose and is punitive in intent. It tests the genuine desperation of families awaiting rehousing. While they hang on, squeezed in with their parents, or friends, or cramped in tiny bedsits, they have no chance of getting a flat, with waiting lists growing and available housing shrinking. Making life hell for these homeless people is supposed to act as a deterrent against others throwing themselves on the

mercy of the local authorities. Like the workhouses of old, these hotels keep the poor from freezing to death in the streets, but they keep them so miserably that only the utterly destitute would avail themselves of this form of state aid.

16 It is an immensely expensive way to house people atrociously and the cost is rocketing as the number of people in bed and breakfasts grows. In London alone the boroughs spent £4.3 millions on bed and breakfast in 1982. This rose last year to £6 millions—money pointlessly thrown away, enriching the hotel proprietors grotesquely, as it debilitates the housing budgets of the boroughs. It is accounting madness, since that money would pay for housing those people in flats permanently. A private person paying that much rent a week would do the wise thing, borrow money for a mortgage, and pay for a capital asset, that will last for several generations. The Government's obsession with preventing borrowing means throwing away money in a way that no-one would advise for any individual family.

17 Meanwhile, 136,000 houses stand empty in London alone, boroughs deprived of the money to renovate them, falling into worse repair year by year. The housing crisis deepens. The government has cut housing expenditure by two-thirds, while half a million new homes are needed. Housing has gone cold as a political issue, since the early heady days of Shelter and Cathy Come Home, yet the numbers of homeless multiply year after year. 'Do they know, do you think, do they really know what it's like living here?' said one distraught mother. 'I have to think they don't, otherwise what sort of people are they?'

Polly Toynbee

1. (a) Look at paragraph one. What made the hotel *seem* respectable? (2)

   (b) According to paragraphs two and three, what was the *real purpose* of this hotel and others like it in London? (2)

2. Read paragraphs four and five.
Point out *FOUR* ways in which these hotels are injurious to their residents' physical and mental health. Give evidence from the passage to support your ideas. (8)

3. Using information from the passage as a whole, describe the *types of people* who find themselves homeless and forced to live in these hotels. (8)

4. How does Sheila differ from other women in her attitude to her predicament? (5)

5. (a) Look at paragraph nine. What is the councils' attitude to their homeless? (2)

   (b) According to paragraph sixteen, what financial criticism can be made of the councils' housing policy? (3)

6. Polly Toynbee compares these hotels to workhouses. Explain what she means by this and by the phrase 'punitive in intent'. (4)

7. Using evidence from the passage as a whole, say what Polly Toynbee's attitude is to the homeless people she describes. How, do you think, are we as readers intended to respond to this article? (4)

8. What does the drawing add, if anything, to the effectiveness of this article? (2)

40 Marks

PAPER 1 EXPRESSION

Section A

A1 Royalty

A2 Youth Activities

A3 Political Candidates

Section B

Essays

PAPER 2 UNDERSTANDING

Comprehension A:

It's Just the Way It Is by H.E. Bates

Comprehension B:

The Capital Punishment Debate

Paper 1, Section A

A1. Royalty

*Below are several comments about the role of Royalty in our society. Look at them closely, then write an **essay** saying what **your** views are on this subject. You **must** refer to at least **some** of the views here but you must also **add** some of your own.*

Member of the Public
'They work hard, have very little privacy and always have to keep up a certain image.'

A Working Man
'Some of them seem to get a lot of money for what they do. I don't mind the Queen and Prince Charles having a decent income.'

Royalist
'My life is very ordinary, cooking and cleaning for a husband and three growing children. Reading about the Royal Family, looking at their beautiful clothes, learning about their expensive life style and trying to imagine what their fairy-tale castles and palaces are like inside, all help me to escape from routine. We all need some fantasy in our lives; they provide it!'

Anti-Royalist
'The monarchy should be abolished. It is too expensive for the nation to keep.'

Student
'They have privileges which they don't even earn. They get them only through birth.'

Member of the Tourist Board
'The members of the Royal Family, all of them, are good ambassadors for our country. People come from all over the world to see where they live and to try to get a glimpse of them. What a marvellous boost they give to our tourist industry.'

American
'I'd rather have the Royal Family than a President any day!'

Trade Union Official
'The gap between them and ordinary people is far too wide. Why should they be able to have all those palaces, so much land and be able to fly off to warm countries whenever they want? There are so many people in our country who don't have a home and who can never look forward to a holiday. It isn't fair!'

Paper 1, Section A

A2. Youth Activities

Below are printed some facts about

1. The Scout Association and the Girl Guides Association
2. Youth Clubs
3. The Duke of Edinburgh's Award Scheme

After carefully reading these facts, write an essay stating which one you would prefer to be involved in and why. You must also say why you would reject the other two and give reasons.

1. The Scout Association and the Girl Guides Association

These two organisations, which are very similar, have been described as the biggest and happiest free associations for young people that the world has ever known. Robert Baden Powell began the movements early this century.

HERE ARE JUST A FEW FACTS ABOUT THEM.

(i) Scouts and Guides wear uniforms and pay subs.

(ii) Membership is voluntary and is open to young people without racial or religious discrimination, as long as they obey their Law and make their Promise.

(iii) This Promise involves putting service for God first, serving one's country and one's fellow citizens and keeping the Scout or Guide Law.

(iv) Neither movement is involved in political activity.

(v) Both movements have an educational purpose, which is basically to develop individual character.

(vi) Their motto is 'Be Prepared'.

(vii) Scouts and Guides work for badges, such as Airman and Boatman badges for the Scouts; Hostess and Music Lover for the Guides.

(viii) Scouts and Guides can work for their Duke of Edinburgh's Award within their organisation.

(ix) Scouts and Guides are divided into groups called patrols, with a patrol leader and a patrol second.

(x) Emphasis is placed on group work, in patrols, on giving individuals responsibility and on developing a strong competitive element.

(xi) Both movements work within a framework, or programme, 'though there is flexibility within the framework. In Guides for instance, a programme is devised to help a girl to mature by providing opportunities for her to develop her:

Mind
Relationships with other people
Physical Fitness
Readiness and Ability to Serve Others
Character
Homecraft Skills
Creative Ability
Enjoyment of the Outdoors

A Handbook is provided explaining ways in which this Eight Point Programme might be carried out.

2. Youth Clubs

(i) Youth club members do not wear uniforms and they do not work for badges or other targets.

(ii) Generally members pay subs.

(iii) Leaders do not have a title; their work is largely voluntary, though some youth leaders are paid.

(iv) There is no hierarchy in a youth club, as in Scouts and Guides e.g. Chief Scout, Patrol Leader, Patrol Second etc.

(v) Usually a Committee, elected by members of the club, meets and draws up rules on issues such as smoking, payment of subs, activities etc.

(vi) Emphasis is placed on the individual, who can choose to take part in many activities, varying from youth club to youth club. These might include:

Table tennis	Judo
Pool	Treasure hunts
Badminton	Discussions
Weight Lifting	Basketball
Darts	Quizzes
Dancing	Readings
Canoeing	Videos and Slide Shows
Hiking	Talks

(vii) Youth clubs aim to provide an opportunity for young people to communicate together. They help to make members aware of other people's needs, particularly in the local community.

(viii) The organisation of a youth club is very flexible. There is no strict framework; members can come and go as they wish.

(ix) Church youth clubs aim to introduce their members to a Christian way of life.

(x) Members can work for their Duke of Edinburgh's Award within their organisation.

3. The Duke of Edinburgh's Award Scheme

(i) The scheme is not itself a youth organisation. It is run through youth clubs, schools, industrial firms, the Armed Forces and Government Departments.

(ii) It is voluntary and a small entrance fee has to be paid. There is no uniform.

(iii) It is non-competitive and individual, so the Award is within the reach of all who take part.

(iv) The scheme encourages enterprise, self-discipline, a lot of effort and most important of all *SELF-RELIANCE* and a sense of responsibility to others.

(v) The successful person will receive a badge and a certificate along with the satisfaction of completing the stated requirements.

(vi) There are *three* separate Awards: Bronze, Silver and Gold. The minimum starting ages for each Award are:

Bronze	—	14 years
Silver	—	15 years
Gold	—	16 years

(vii) Here is the framework of the Scheme: In order to qualify for each Award, all those taking part have to qualify in *four* sections. These are:

Service—to encourage service to others
Expeditions—to encourage a sense of adventure and discovery
Skills—to encourage the discovery and development of personal interests and social and practical skills
Physical Recreation—to encourage participation in physical recreation and improvement of performance.

(viii) Each person taking part has to keep a Record Book, which should record personal progress through the Scheme and be signed at each stage by adult testers.

(ix) Guidance through each stage is given by an adult or adults who are knowledgeable about particular activities.

Paper 1, Section A

A3. Political Candidates

Because of ill-health, a member of Clayton Borough Council has resigned and a bye-election is to be held to fill the vacancy. The vacant seat is for Brooklands ward which has a population of approximately 2,000. The ward is in the centre of Clayton (total population 38,000) and includes the main shopping area and some private and council housing.

The three candidates for the vacancy are:

Keith Jones, Age 25. Married with two small daughters. Self-employed taxi driver. Does not live in Brooklands ward but has an office there. Lives on outskirts of Clayton.

Joan Shaw, Age 43. Married with three teenage children. Health Visitor. Works in Brooklands ward. Lives in a village three miles outside Clayton, but still within the Clayton Borough Council local government area.

Mohammed Patel, Age 50. Married with four children in their late teens and early twenties. Runs a grocery shop in Brooklands ward. Lives over his shop.

Read the list of Clayton's chief problems and the excerpts from the electoral addresses, which each of the three candidates made, and then decide which one YOU would vote for if you were a resident in Brooklands ward.

Give reasons for your choice and explain why you did not choose the other two. If you feel you would not vote for any of these candidates, explain why you would reject each one AND describe the kind of councillor you would vote for.

Clayton's Problems

—A high unemployment level, especially among young people
—Vandalism and petty crime
—Recreational facilities in need of repair, renewal and augmentation
—Inadequate council housing, much of it old and in need of modernisation
—An ageing population
—Litter

Keith Jones

As a firm believer in private enterprise, I feel that the best way to help the unemployed of Clayton is to provide them with the facilities to become self-employed. I would like to see Clayton Borough Council purchase the disused cotton mill situated in Brooklands ward near the town centre and convert it into 'nursery units' (small workshops), so that people can start their own businesses.

Any increase in the rates must be kept to the minimum and to this end I believe we should encourage those council tenants who can afford it to buy their own homes.

If people are to be encouraged to come into Clayton town centre to shop, then it is our duty to provide good car-parking facilities.

Joan Shaw

A sizeable increase in the rates is essential if we are to maintain and improve Clayton's amenities. The young and the old alike need a well-equipped community centre in Brooklands ward—a place which can provide recreational facilities for the under fives, teenagers and the elderly.

Let us make the centre of our town more attractive and so encourage civic pride by planting trees and flowering shrubs. Our parks should be improved too. For those with time on their hands, more allotments should be provided.

Many of our elderly citizens live in fear of vandals and petty thieves. Better street lighting and the provision of specially designed, sheltered accommodation should help allay some of the fears our senior citizens have.

We definitely need more new council houses, but we should also build a few new shops, which can be leased at fair rents to enable some of our unemployed to set up in business.

Mohammed Patel

Brooklands ward, the heart of Clayton, needs a great deal of improvement.

Let us establish a pedestrian precinct in the main shopping area and provide pelican crossings over the two major roads, which cut through the centre of the town. Many people have suffered serious injury as the result of cars travelling too fast on these roads. Surely it is time that this problem was tackled properly?

At night time Brooklands is a magnet for young vandals. What we need is better street lighting, which is also vandal-proof.

Thoughtless people allow their dogs to wander at will through the streets and to foul the pavements. No one would want to come shopping in Clayton town centre until this problem is solved by appointing a Dog Warden.

Young people who have no employment need excellent facilities for sports and games to help them to keep fit and to spend their time positively. What we need are more pitches for football, hockey and cricket to be created in the park near the town centre.

If we also built a swimming pool and a running track, apart from providing facilities for our youngsters, they would attract visitors to the town.

Paper 1, Section B

Write about two sides on ONE of the following. Your aim, remember, is to produce an imaginative and lively piece of writing.

B1. Read this letter, written to a newspaper:

'I'm sometimes an adult. Sometimes not.

I can't have a holiday abroad as a child, since with most companies 12 is the relevant year.

I can't drink in a public house, at least until I'm 18, but I could well be charged full train fare at 16.

I even find that there are variations in practice in different districts in relation to transport.

And cinemas are a nightmare.

Why not let's rationalise and make the full rate apply —and everything connected with it—when we are 16.

This would be a relief compared with our present chaos.'

STUART McFARLANE, aged 15, Glasgow

At what age do you think you should be regarded as an adult and why?

B2. The envelope, containing your examination results, is there on the floor by the letter box. Describe your feelings before, during and after opening the envelope.

B3. The Fairground.

B4. A newspaper report stated:

'Two climbers were rescued from the Cairngorms, as gales, sleet and snow caused hazardous conditions in Scotland.'

Imagine you were in the rescue team. Describe the part you played and give your personal view about people who take unnecessary risks in such bad weather conditions.

B5. Monarch for a day.

B6. Describe your best—and your worst—days at school.

B7.
'I am ...'   Weave these four statements
'I love ...'   into a description of yourself.
'I hate ...'
'I believe ...'

B8. Fear!

B9. Describe what happened when a special occasion was spoilt by rain.

B10. Study the photograph and write about it in any way you like.

Paper 2, Comprehension A

Read the short story below and then answer the questions which follow.

It's Just The Way It Is by **H E Bates** from 'The Stories of Flying Officer X'
(Jonathan Cape)

November rain falls harshly on the clean tarmac, and the wind, turning suddenly, lifts sprays of yellow elm leaves over the black hangars.

The man and the woman, escorted by a sergeant, look very small as they walk by the huge cavernous opening where the bombers are.

The man, who is perhaps fifty and wears a black overcoat and bowler hat, holds an umbrella slantwise over the woman, who is about the same age, but very grey and slow on her feet, so that she is always a pace or two behind the umbrella and must bend her face against the rain.

On the open track beyond the hangars they are caught up by the wind, and are partially blown along, huddled together. Now and then the man looks up at the Stirlings, which protrude over the track, but he looks quickly away again and the woman does not look at all.

'Here we are, sir,' the sergeant says at last. The man says 'Thank you,' but the woman does not speak.

They have come to a long one-storeyed building, painted grey, with 'Squadron Headquarters' in white letters on the door. The sergeant opens the door for them and they go in, the man flapping and shaking the umbrella as he closes it down.

The office of the Wing Commander is at the end of a passage; the sergeant taps on the door, opens it and salutes. As the man and woman follow him, the man first, taking off his hat, the woman hangs a little behind, her face passive.

'Mr and Mrs Shepherd, sir,' the sergeant says.

'Oh yes, good afternoon.' The sergeant, saluting, closes the door and goes.

'Good afternoon, sir,' the man says.

The woman does not speak.

'Won't you please sit down, madam?' the Wing Commander says. 'And you too, sir. Please sit down.'

He pushes forward two chairs, and slowly the man and the woman sit down, the man leaning his weight on the umbrella.

The office is small and there are no more chairs. The Wing Commander remains standing, his back resting against a table, beyond which, on the wall, the flight formations are ticketed up.

He is quite young, but his eyes, which are glassy and grey, seem old and focused distantly so that he seems to see far beyond the grey-green Stirlings lined up on the dark tarmac in the rain. He folds his arms across his chest and is glad at last when the man looks up at him and speaks.

'We had your letter, sir. But we felt we should like to come and see you, too.'

'I am glad you came.'

'I know you are busy, but we felt we must come. We felt you wouldn't mind.'

'Not at all. People often come.'

'There are just some things we should like to ask you.'

'I understand.'

The man moves his lips, ready to speak again, but the words do not come. For a moment his lips move like those of someone who stutters, soundlessly, quite helplessly. His hands grip hard on the handle of the umbrella, but still the words do not come and at last it is the Wing Commander who speaks.

'You want to know if everything possible was done to eliminate an accident?'

The man looks surprised that someone should know this, and can only nod his head.

'Everything possible was done.'

'Thank you, sir.'

'But there are things you can never foresee. The weather forecast may say, for example, no cloud over Germany, for perhaps sixteen hours, but you go over and you find a thick layer of cloud all the way, and you never see your target—and perhaps there is severe icing as you come home.'

'Was it like this when ...'

'Something like it. You never know. You can't be certain.'

Suddenly, before anyone can speak again, the engines of a Stirling close by are revved up to a roar that seems to shake the walls of the room; and the woman looks up, startled, as if terrified that the 'plane will race forward and crash against the windows. The roar of airscrews rises furiously and then falls again, and the sudden rise and fall of sound seems to frighten her into speech.

'Why aren't you certain? Why can't you be certain? He should never have gone out! You must know that! You must know it! You must know that he should never have gone!'

'Please,' the man says.

'Day after day you are sending out young boys like this. Young boys who haven't begun to live. Young boys who don't know what life is. Day after day you send them out and they don't come back and you don't care! You don't care!'

She is crying bitterly now and the man puts his arm on her shoulder. She is wearing a fur and he draws it a fraction closer about her neck.

'You don't care, do you! You don't care! It doesn't matter to you. You don't care!'

'Mother,' the man says.

Arms folded, the Wing Commander looks at the floor, silently waiting for her to stop. She goes on for a minute or more longer, shouting and crying her words, violent and helpless, until at last she is exhausted and stops. Her fur slips off her shoulder and falls to the ground, and the man picks it up and holds it in his hands, helpless, too.

The Wing Commander walks over to the window and looks out. The airscrews of the Stirling are turning smoothly, shining like steel pin-wheels in the rain, and now, with the woman no longer shouting, the room seems very silent, and finally the Wing Commander walks back across the room and stands in front of the man and woman again.

'You came to ask me something,' he says.

'Take no notice, sir. Please. She is upset.'

'You want to know what happened? Isn't that it?'

'Yes, sir. It would help us a little, sir.'

The Wing Commander says very quietly: 'Perhaps I can tell you a little. He was always coming to me and asking to go out on operations. Most of them do that. But he used to come and beg to be allowed to go more than most.

So more often than not it was a question of stopping him from going rather than making him go. It was a question of holding him back. You see?'

'Yes, sir.'

'And whenever I gave him a trip he was very happy. And the crew were happy. They liked going with him. They liked being together, with him, because they liked him so much and they trusted him. There were seven of them and they were all together.'

The woman is listening, slightly lifting her head.

'It isn't easy to tell you what happened on that trip. But we know that conditions got suddenly very bad and that there was bad cloud for a long way. And we know that they had navigational difficulties and that they got a long way off their course.

'Even that might not have mattered, but as they were coming back the outer port engine went. Then the radio transmitter went and the receiver. Everything went wrong. The wireless operator somehow got the transmitter and the receiver going again, but then they ran short of petrol. You see, everything was against him.'

'Yes, sir.'

'They came back the last hundred miles at about a thousand feet. But they trusted him completely, and he must have known they trusted him. A crew gets like that—flying together gives them this tremendous faith in each other.'

'Yes, sir.'

'They trusted him to get them home, and he got them home. Everything was against him. He feathered the outer starboard engine and then, in spite of everything, got them down on two engines. It was a very good show. A very wonderful show.'

The man is silent, but the woman lifts her head. She looks at the Wing Commander for a moment or two, immobile, very steady, and then says, quite distinctly, 'Please tell us the rest.'

'There is not much,' he says. 'It was a very wonderful flight, but they were out of luck. They were up against all the bad luck in the world. When they came to land they couldn't see the flarepath very well, but he got them down. And then, as if they hadn't had enough, they came down slightly off the runway and hit an obstruction. Even then they didn't crash badly. But it must have thrown him and he must have hit his head somewhere with great force, and that was the end.'

'Yes, sir. And the others?' the man says.

'They were all right. Even the second pilot. I wish you could have talked to them. It would have helped if you could have talked to them. They know that he brought them home. They know that they owe everything to him.'

'Yes, sir.'

The Wing Commander does not speak, and the man very slowly puts the fur over the woman's shoulders. It is like a signal for her to get up, and as she gets to her feet the man stands up too, straightening himself, no longer leaning on the umbrella.

'I haven't been able to tell you much,' the Wing Commander says. 'It's just the way it is.'

'It's everything,' the man says.

For a moment the woman still does not speak, but now she stands quite erect. Her eyes are quite clear, and her lips, when she does speak at last, are quite calm and firm.

'I know now that we all owe something to him,' she says. 'Goodbye.'

'Goodbye, madam.'

'Goodbye, sir,' the man says.

'You are all right for transport?'

'Yes, sir. We have a taxi.'

'Good. The sergeant will take you back.'

'Goodbye, sir. Thank you.'

'Goodbye,' the woman says.

'Goodbye.'

They go out of the office. The sergeant meets them at the outer door, and the man puts up the umbrella against the rain. They walk away along the wet perimeter, dwarfed once again by the grey-green noses of the Stirlings. They walk steadfastly, almost proudly, and the man holds the umbrella a little higher than before, and the woman, keeping up with him now, lifts her head.

And the Wing Commander, watching them from the window, momentarily holds his face in his hands.

It's Just the Way It Is by **H E Bates**

1. (a) Where is the setting of this story?   (2)

   (b) What are the Stirlings?   (2)

2. Why do the man and woman look small?   (2)

3. Why have the couple come to meet the Wing Commander?   (3)

4. (a) After being so quiet, what seems to motivate the woman to speak out?
                                                                                (3)

   (b) She verbally attacks the Wing Commander. What does she say to him?
                                                                                (5)

5. What does the Wing Commander say to the couple in reply to the outburst? Use your own words if you can.   (6)

6. From reading this story, what kind of a man does the Wing Commander seem to be?   (6)

7. (a) Describe the reaction of the couple to the Wing Commander's story. (3)

   (b) Why are their responses and movements so different from the beginning of the story?   (4)

8. Why do you think the Wing Commander held his face in his hands? (Last line.)   (2)

9. What is the significance of the title?   (2)

40 Marks

Paper 2, Comprehension B

Read the following article and answer the questions on it in your own words.

The Capital Punishment Debate

The United States, along with South Africa and Russia, is one of the major white-ruled countries that still executes people. Hanging, shooting, electrocution or poisoning are the various penalties imposed in about three-quarters of the United States, where there are about 20,000 murders a year. Of these, roughly 28% are unsolved. The U.S. Justice Department has estimated that there may be at large about three dozen people who repeatedly commit murders. These 'serial killers' are believed to criss-cross the country, killing, for no obvious reason, in the towns they visit.

Meanwhile, on the death rows of 38 states, close on 1,200 of those apprehended and convicted for killing await their fate. Only a handful of executions has been carried out since the Supreme Court reinstated the death penalty in 1976, after abolishing it four years previously. The great majority of executions are delayed because Americans are uneasy about what should happen to condemned prisoners. According to a poll in 1983, two thirds of Americans favour capital punishment, believing that it has a deterrent effect, yet they are concerned that it should be socially acceptable. The result is that appeals against sentence are allowed to drag on for years whilst fine distinctions between capital and non-capital offences are pursued in the courts.

Here in Britain, the last execution was carried out in 1964 and the death penalty was abolished in November 1965. Nearly twenty years later, however, there are those who would like capital punishment reintroduced. In a poll held in Britain (MORI June 1981) seventy-eight per cent of those interviewed said that they would like to see certain crimes such as terrorist murders, the murder of a policeman and the murder of a kidnap victim carry the death penalty.

There is no doubt that homicide (the term covers murder, manslaughter and infanticide) is on the increase in Britain. Official figures show that in 1981 there were nearly six hundred killings and that the total number of offences initially regarded as homicide between 1971 and 1981 is fifty per cent higher than in the period between 1962 and 1971. Over the same period, the number of serious offences against the person increased by about fifty-five per cent. In most murder cases in Britain, the victims are closely associated with the suspects and are killed for personal or emotional reasons, frequently out of rage or jealousy or drunken desperation.

The British pro-hanging lobby argue that the death penalty would have a deterrent effect on specific categories of homicide, such as acts of terrorism and the murder of policemen. They claim that capital punishment is swift and sure and signifies society's total abhorrence of certain sorts of offences. In support of their case, they seize on the statistical evidence that between 1971 and 1981, twenty-eight people previously convicted of homicide killed again.

The abolitionists, on the other hand, point out that hanging is too simplistic a solution for the complex problems associated with homicide. Many of them believe that the taking of life is immoral and that it is unnecessary to demonstrate by capital punishment that killing is wrong, especially as a form of communal retribution. Imprisonment is sufficient to protect the public. They too make use of statistics to strengthen their case. There have been a significant number of murder cases since 1945 in which justice has miscarried or in which grave doubts about the correctness of the 'guilty' verdict persist. In some of these cases those mistakenly found guilty were hanged, whilst, in others, there is a strong probability that they would have been hanged had capital punishment been a sentence available to the courts. In 1981, about 3,800 people previously convicted of homicide at some time during the preceding thirty years were alive and at liberty in England and Wales.

Whether the death penalty will ever be reintroduced in Britain remains to be seen, but research studies carried out in Britain, in the United States and on an international basis for the United Nations, show that there is no statistical evidence that the abolition of the death penalty has increased the rate of homicide or that its restoration has ever led to a fall in the rate.

1. Name two countries mentioned in the passage which have retained the death penalty. (2)

2. Why, despite the very large number of condemned prisoners, are so few executions carried out in the United States? (2)

3. It is almost twenty years since the death penalty was abolished in Britain. Why, according to the passage, has there been a call for its reintroduction? (3)

4. According to the second and third paragraphs of the passage, how does public opinion in the United States compare with public opinion in Britain with regard to capital punishment? (3)

5. What differences are there between the number and nature of homicides in Britain and the U.S.A.? (5)

6. Write out, in the form of a set of notes, the arguments *FOR* and the arguments *AGAINST* the reintroduction of capital punishment in Britain. You should use only the information given in the passage. (12)

7. In your own words, explain the conclusions of the research into the effectiveness of the death penalty as a deterrent. (3)

8. There are a number of other arguments, not mentioned in the passage, which might be advanced in favour of or against the death penalty. What are they? Write about a side giving your views on capital punishment. (You may use some of the information included here, if you wish, but at least half your answer must consist of your own ideas.) (10)

40 Marks

PAPER 1 EXPRESSION

Section A

A1 Heroes and Heroines

A2 A Trip to London

A3 Getting Around

Section B

Essays

PAPER 2 UNDERSTANDING

Comprehension A:

A Minority by Frank O'Connor

Comprehension B:

Pocket Money

Paper 1, Section A

A1. Heroes and Heroines

*Read the extracts below. Referring to at least **some** of these comments, describe **your own** thoughts about what heroes and heroines mean to you.*

Teacher
'My heroines are Jane Austen and the Brontë sisters. They were women who had the ability to observe life and create great literature out of their experience and imagination.'

Cancer Research Fund-raiser
'Pat Seed is my heroine. Herself a cancer victim, she was a selfless campaigner for cancer research and raised over £1,000,000 for a scanner to detect cancer in its early stages.'

Amateur Footballer
'One day I want to play football like Kevin Keegan. He's the best footballer there's ever been. And he's a good sportsman, not like some famous people in sport who are paid a fortune and then have tantrums when the game's not going their way.'

Fifth-former
'When people ask me who my favourite pop star is, I say Tracey Ullman. She makes great records and she makes me laugh. We're always taking her off at school.'

Sixteen Year Old
'My dad's my hero. He's gentle, kind, caring and protective. When I feel everyone is against me, my dad is always there, encouraging me and supporting me.'

Local Councillor
'I cannot help admiring a man in our neighbourhood, David Simpson, who spends so much of his spare time helping others. He organises the local cub pack, runs in marathons to raise money for charity and makes sure that the gardens of five elderly people are kept neat and tidy. He's been doing this for years.'

Housewife
'My respect and admiration go to those skilful surgeons who specialise in organ transplants and whose work gives men and women a new lease of life.'

Paper 1, Section A

A2. A Trip to London

*On Saturday, 20th April, a party of pupils and teachers from Kennet High School, went on a day trip to London. Printed below are extracts from the diaries of three pupils, recording some of the events of the day. Read them carefully and using at least **some** of the information given in them, write an **article** about the trip for your school or college magazine. You may of course, use additional information **of your own**.*

From the diary of Mike Lloyd

20TH APRIL. SATURDAY. Coach should have left 7 a.m.—bit late—forgot my sandwiches. In spite of this and John Danby being sick in coach, still arrived 10.30. From coach, went via underground to Trafalgar Square, fed pigeons, walked down Mall to Buckingham Palace, through St. James's Park to Horse Guards' Parade, through to Downing Street, into Whitehall and then down to the Houses of Parliament. Apart from a short stop in St. James's Park to eat picnic, we hadn't stopped. So by the time we reached the Houses of Parliament, my feet were nearly dropping off. We were glad to sit down. Later we were allowed to go to Oxford Street, but John, Phil and I got lost in the crowds and we nearly didn't make it to the theatre. Saw the show 'Cats'. Fantastic! Then back home on the coach; slept all the way. What a day! My mum liked my new tee-shirt.

From the diary of Polly Green

20TH APRIL. SATURDAY. I awoke feeling so excited for this was to be no ordinary Saturday. I was going to London for the first time. Although I was early at the coach, some were late, much to the teachers' annoyance. In spite of the late start we arrived in London at 10.30 as planned. The sun shone, the sky was blue and the flowering cherries were in full bloom. It was fun feeding the pigeons in Trafalgar Square. Some people spent a lot of money on birdseed. I couldn't believe how tame the pigeons were as they perched on our hands, shoulders and heads. I took lots of photographs, especially outside Buckingham Palace where I was one of the few lucky enough to see the Queen driving out in a big, black shiny car. I thought the Palace was too grey and dismal, but it was exciting seeing the Queen. In the afternoon, we had some free time, so four of us went on a boat trip on the Thames, as far as St. Paul's Cathedral and back. That was a real treat and a bonus for we had not expected to see so much in one day. Before returning home, we saw the famous musical 'Cats'. It was a fast moving, exciting show and well worth seeing. The costumes were out of this world. We arrived home exhausted but very happy. It had been a day to remember.

From the diary of Katie Paterson

SATURDAY, 20TH APRIL. Went to London again today. Journey boring apart from meeting a nice lad at second stop on motorway. Glad we weren't in school uniform; too warm. Wore my new top and jeans—Joanne liked them. Saw the Queen; never done that before. I'm sure she smiled specially at me. Enjoyed 'Cats' but it was very noisy. Allowed some free time so went to Oxford Street. Miss Clarke nearly had kittens when three out of our class didn't turn up in time for the show. Mr Norman had to wait outside until they turned up. I liked the Houses of Parliament, especially lit up, but it's hard to believe that 10, Downing Street is where the Prime Minister lives. Saw lots of lads sunbathing in the Park where we had our sandwiches. Enjoyed seeing the soldiers changing the Guard. The sing-song on the way home was great.

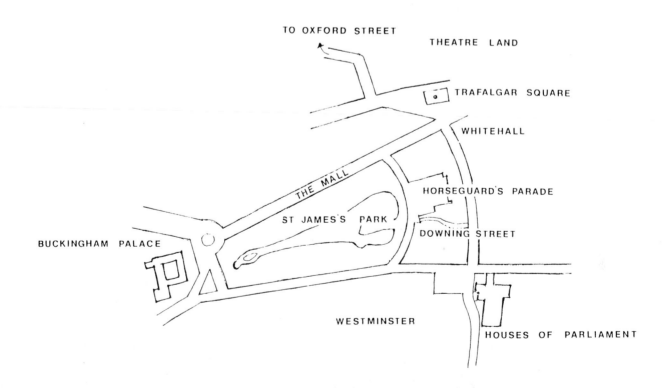

Paper 1, Section A

A3. Getting Around

Study the drawings and the following facts about each of the three forms of transport. Then, using this and any other information of your own, describe the advantages and disadvantages of EACH ONE. Finally, say which you would prefer, giving reasons for your choice.

TABLE

	BICYCLE	MOTOR BIKE	CAR
Initial Cost	£98 (new)	£555 (new)	£500 (second hand)
Road Tax	none	£9	£90
Approx. cost of annual insurance	none	£45 (Third Party, Fire & Theft)	£180 (Third Party, Fire & Theft)
Minimum legal age	not applicable	16	17
Cost of test	none	£14.40	£14.40
Cost of tuition	none	minimum 10 hours on & off road £37 in all	£7-£9 per hour
Cost of licence	none	£10	£10
M.P.G.	none	200	40
Total road accidents 1981 (Adults)	26,496	(Including mopeds & motor scooters) 70,949	256,531
Fatal & Serious Casualties 1981	3,393	(Including mopeds & motor scooters) 22,778	33,625

Paper 1, Section B

Write about two sides on ONE of the following. Remember your aim should be to produce an imaginative and lively piece of writing.

B1. You applied for and were offered ONE of these posts advertised in your local newspaper. Describe your first day.

OFFICE JUNIOR Required If you are young, lively and with an extremely outgoing personality—then you are the person we are looking for. Promising career prospects for the right individual.	DRIVER SALESPERSON/ STORES MALE/FEMALE required, preferably with commercial vehicle spares experience
WANTED TECHNICIAN/ ELECTRICIAN To assist contracts engineer/management	YOUNG PERSON required for town centre ladies' fashion shop, also to assist in warehouse. Prospects of promotion for suitable applicant.

B2. Describe someone you know who is very popular and account for his or her popularity.

B3. Parents.

B4. At five o'clock one evening, your aunt telephones inviting you to join her and her family on a fortnight's holiday *the following day*. (One of the original members of the party has had to drop out.) You accept the invitation.

Describe your feelings and hurried preparations for this, your first trip away from your own family.

B5. The First Time.

B6. 'I didn't really mean to do it. It was an accident!' Describe a time when you said this.

B7. Hope.

B8. A long, hot summer's day.

B9. The Agreement.

B10. Look carefully at these photographs and write about them in any way you like.

Paper 2, Comprehension A

Read the short story below and then answer the questions which follow.

A Minority by **Frank O'Connor** from 'Collection Three' (Macmillan)

Denis Halligan noticed Willy Stein for the first time one Sunday when the other fellows were at Mass. As Denis was a Protestant, he didn't go to Mass. Instead, he sat on the steps outside the chapel with Willy. Willy was a thin, seedy little chap with long, wild hair. It was an autumn morning; there was
5. mist on the trees, and you could scarcely see the great ring of mountains that cut them off there in the middle of Ireland, miles from anywhere.

'Why did they send you here if you're a Proddy?' asked Willy.

'I don't know,' said Denis, who felt his background was so queer that he didn't want to explain it to anybody. 'I suppose because it was cheap.'
10. 'Is your old fellow a Catholic?' asked Willy.

'No,' replied Denis. 'Is yours?'

'No,' Willy said contemptuously. 'He was a Proddy. My old one was a Proddy, too.'

'Where do they live?' asked Denis.
15. 'They're dead,' Willy said, making the motion of spitting. 'The bloody Germans killed them.'

'Oh, cripes!' Denis said regretfully. Denis had a great admiration for everything German, particularly tank generals, and when he grew up he wanted to be a tank general himself, but it seemed a pity that they had to kill
20. Willy's father and mother. Bad as it was to have your parents separated, as his own were, it was worse having them dead. 'Was it a bomb?' he asked.

'No,' Willy replied without undue emotion. 'They were killed in a camp. They sent me over to the Cumminses in Dublin or I'd have been killed too. The Cumminses are Catholics. That's why I was sent here.'
25. 'Do you like it here?' asked Denis.

'I do not,' Willy said scornfully in his Dublin accent, and then took out a slingshot and fitted a stone in it. 'I'd sooner Vienna. Vienna was gas. When I grow up I'm going get out of this blooming place.'

'But what will you do?'
30. 'Aw, go to sea, or something. I don't care.'

Denis was interested in Willy. Apart from the fact that they were the only Proddies in the school, Willy struck him as being really tough, and Denis admired toughness. He was always trying to be tough himself, but there was a soft streak in him that kept breaking out. It was breaking out now, and he
35. knew it. Though he saw that Willy didn't give a rap about his parents, Denis couldn't help being sorry for him, alone in the middle of Ireland with his father and mother dead half a world away. He said as much to his friend Nigel Healy, from Cork, that afternoon, but Nigel only gave a superior sniff.

'But that fellow is mad,' he said, in his reasonable way.
40. 'How is he mad?' asked Denis.

'He's not even left go home on holidays,' explained Nigel. 'He has to stay here all during the summer. Those people were nice to him, and what does he do? Breaks every window in the place. They had the police to the house twice. He's mad on slingshots.'
45. 'He had one this morning,' said Denis.

'Last time he was caught with one he got flogged,' said Nigel. 'You see, the fellow has no sense. I even saw him putting sugar on his meat.'

'But why did he do that?' asked Denis.

'Said he liked it,' replied Nigel with a smile and a shrug. 'He's bound to
50. get expelled one of these days. You'd want to mind yourself with him.'

But for some reason that only made Denis more interested in Willy Stein,
and he looked forward to meeting him again by himself the following Sunday.
He was curious to know why the Germans would want to kill Stein's father
and mother. That seemed to him a funny thing to do—unless, of course, they
55. were spies for the English.

Again they sat on the steps, but this morning the sun was warm and bright,
and the mountains all round them were a brilliant blue. If Stein's parents were
really spies, the idea of it did not seem to have occurred to him. According
to him, his father had been a lawyer and his mother something on a news-
60. paper, and he didn't seem to remember much about them except that they
were both 'gas'. Everything with Stein was 'gas'. His mother was gentle and
timid, and let him have everything he wanted, so she was 'great gas'. His
father was sure she was ruining him, and was always on to him to study and
be better than other kids, and when his father got like that he used to weep
65. and shout and wave his hands, but that was only now and then. He was gas,
too, though not, Denis gathered, great gas. Willy suddenly waved his hands
and shouted something in a foreign language.

'What's that?' asked Denis with the deepest admiration.

70. 'German,' Stein replied, in his graceless way.

'What does it mean?' asked Denis.

'I dunno,' Stein said lightly.

Denis was disappointed. For a fellow like himself, who was interested in
tanks, a spatter of German might one day be useful. He had the impression
75. that Stein was only letting on to remember parents he had lost before he was
really old enough to remember them.

Their talk was interrupted by Father Houlihan, a tall, morose-looking
priest. He had a bad belly and a worse temper, but Denis knew Father
Houlihan liked him, and he admired Father Houlihan. He was violent, but
80. he wasn't a stinker.

'Hah!' he said, in his mocking way. 'And what do you two cock sparrows
think you're doing out here?'

'We're excused, Father,' Denis said brightly, leaping to his feet.

'No one is excused anything in this place till I excuse him,' snarled Father
85. Houlihan cheerfully, 'and I don't excuse much. Run into Mass now, ye pair
of heathens!'

'But we're Protestants, Father!' Stein cried, and Denis was half afraid of
seeing the red flush on Father Houlihan's forehead that showed he was out
for blood.

90. 'Aha, what fine Protestants we have in ye!' he snorted good-humouredly.
'I suppose you have a Protestant slingshot in your pocket at this very minute,
you scoundrel, you!'

'I have not!' Stein shouted. 'You know Murphy took it off me.'

'Mr Murphy to you, Willy Stein,' said the priest, pinching his ear playfully
95. and pushing him towards the chapel. 'And next time I catch you with a
slingshot I'll give you a Catholic cane on your fat Protestant backside.'

The two boys went into chapel and sat together on a bench at the back.
Willy was muttering indignantly to himself, but he waited until everyone was
kneeling with bowed head. Then, to Denis's horror, he took out a slingshot
100. and a bit of paper, which he chewed up into a wet ball. There was nothing
hasty or spontaneous about this. Stein went about it with a concentration that
was almost pious. As the bell rang for the Consecration, there was a *ping*, and

a seminarist kneeling at the side of the chapel put his hand to his ear and looked angrily round. But by this time Stein had thrown himself on his knees,

105. and his eyes were shut in a look of rapt devotion. It gave Denis quite a turn. Even if he wasn't a Catholic, he had been brought up to respect every form of religion.

The business of going to Mass and feeling out of it made Denis Halligan completely fed up with being a Proddy. He had never liked it anyway, even

110. at home, as a kid. He was gregarious, and a born gang leader, a promoter of organisation, and it cut him to the heart to feel that at any moment he might be deserted by his gang because, through no fault of his own, he was not a Catholic and might accidentally say or do the wrong thing. He even resented the quiet persuasion that the school authorities exercised on him. A senior

115. called Hanley, whom Nigel described sarcastically as 'Halligan's angel', was attached to Denis—not to proselytise, but to give him an intelligent under-standing of the religious life of the group. Hanley had previously been attached to Stein, but that had proved hopeless, because Stein seemed to take Hanley's company as a guarantee of immunity from punishment, so he merely

120. involved Hanley in every form of forbidden activity, from smoking to stealing. One day when Stein stole a gold tie-pin from a master's room, Hanley had to report him. On Hanley's account, he was not flogged, but told to put the tie-pin back in the place from which he had taken it. Stein did so,

125. and seized the opportunity to pinch five shillings instead, and this theft was discovered only when someone saw Stein fast asleep in bed with his mouth open and the two half-crowns in his jaw. As Hanley, a sweet and saintly boy, said to Denis, it wasn't Stein's fault. He was just unbalanced.

In any other circumstances Denis would have enjoyed Hanley's attention,

130. but it made him mad to be singled out like this and looked after like some kid who couldn't undo his own buttons.

'Listen, Hanley,' he said angrily one day when he and Nigel were discussing football and Hanley had slipped a little homily into the conversation. 'It's not good preaching at me. It's not my fault that I'm a Proddy.'

135. 'Well, you don't have to be a Proddy if you don't want to be,' Hanley said with a smile. 'Do you?'

'How can I help it?' asked Denis.

'Well, who'd stop you?'

'My mother would, for one.'

140. 'Did you try?'

'What do you mean, Hanley?'

'I mean, why don't you ask her?' Hanley went on, in the same bland way. 'I wouldn't be too sure she wants you to be a Proddy.'

'How could I ask her?'

145. 'You could write. Or phone,' Hanley added hastily, seeing the look on Denis's face at the notion of writing an extra letter. 'Father Houlihan would let you use the telephone, if you asked him. Or I'll ask him, if you like.'

'Do if you want to,' said Denis. 'I don't care.'

He didn't really believe his mother would agree to something he wanted,

150. just like that, but he had no objection to a free telephone call that would enable him to hear her voice again. To his astonishment, she made no difficulty about it.

'Why, of course, darling,' she said sweetly. 'If that's how you feel and Father Houlihan has no objection, I don't mind. You know I only want you

155. to be happy at school.'

It was a colossal relief. Overnight, his whole position in the school changed. He had ceased to be an outsider. He was one of the gang. He might even be

Chief Gang Leader in the course of time. He was a warm-hearted boy, and he had the feeling that by a simple gesture he had conferred an immense
160. benefit on everybody. The only person who didn't seem too enthusiastic was Father Houlihan, but then he was not much of an enthusiast anyway. 'My bold young convert,' he said, pulling Denis's ear, 'I suppose any day now you'll start paying attention to your lessons.'

Yet the moment he had made his decision, he began to feel guilty about
165. young Stein. As has been said, he was not only gregarious, but he was also a born gang leader, and had the feeling that someone might think he had deserted an ally to secure his own advantage. He was suddenly filled with a wild desire to convert Willy as well, so that the pair of them could be received as a group. He saw it as even more of a duty of Willy's than of his own. Willy
170. had been saved from his parents' fate by a good kind Catholic family, and it was the least they could expect that Willy should show his gratitude to them, to the school, and to Ireland.

But Willy seemed to have a deplorable head for theology. All the time they talked Denis had the impression that Willy was only planning some fresh
175. mischief.

'Ah, come on, Willy,' he said authoritatively, 'you don't want to be a blooming old Proddy.'

'I don't want to be a Cat either,' said Willy with a shrug.

'Don't you want to be like the other fellows in the school?'
180. 'Why don't they want to be like me?' asked Stein.

'Because there's only two of us, and there's hundreds of them. And they're right.'

'And if there were hundreds of us and two of them, we'd be right, I suppose?' Stein said with a sneer. 'You want to be like the rest of them. All
185. right, be like the rest of them, but let me alone.'

'I'm only speaking for your own good,' Denis said, getting mad. What really made him mad was the feeling that somehow Stein wasn't speaking to him at all; that inside, he was as lonely and lost as Denis would have been in similar circumstances, and he wouldn't admit to it, wouldn't break down as
190. Denis would have done. What he really wanted to do was to give Stein a sock in the gob, but he knew that even this was no good. Stein was always being beaten, and he always yelled bloody murder, and next day he came back and did the same thing again. Everyone was thinking exclusively of Stein's good, and it always ended up by their beating him, and it never did him any good
195. at all.

Denis confided his difficulties to Hanley, who was also full of concern for Stein's good, but Hanley only smiled sadly and shook his head.

'I know more about that than you do, Denis,' he said, in his fatherly way. 'I'll tell you if you promise not to repeat it to a living soul.'
200. 'What is it?' asked Denis eagerly.

'Promise! Mind, this is serious!'

'Oh, I promise.'

'The fact is that Stein isn't a Proddy at all,' Hanley said sadly.

'But what is he?'
205. 'Stein is a Jew,' Hanley said in a low voice. 'That's why his father and mother were killed. Nobody know that, though.'

'But does Stein know he's a Jew?' Denis asked excitedly.

'No. And mind, we're not supposed to know it, either. Nobody knows it, except the priests and ourselves.'
210. 'But why doesn't somebody tell him?'

'Because if they did, he might blab about it—you know, he's not very smart—and then all the fellows would be jeering at him. Remember, Denis, if you ever mentioned it, Father Houlihan would skin you alive. He says Stein is after suffering enough. He's sorry for Stein. Mind, I'm only warning you.'

215. 'But won't it be awful for him when he finds out?'

'When he's older and has a job, he won't mind it so much,' said Hanley.

But Denis wasn't sure. Somehow, he had an idea that Stein wanted to stay a Proddy simply because that was what his father and mother had been and it was now the only link he had with them, and if someone would just tell him,

220. he wouldn't care so much and would probably become a Catholic, like Denis. Afterwards, when he did find out that everything he had done was mistaken, it might be too late. And this—and the fact that Father Houlihan, whom Denis admired, was also sorry for Willy Stein—increased his feeling of guilt, and he almost wished he hadn't been in such a hurry himself about being

225. converted. Denis wasn't a bright student, but he was a born officer and he would never have deserted his men.

The excitement of his own reception into the Church almost banished the thought of Stein from his mind. On the Sunday he was received he was allowed to sleep late, and Murphy, the seminarist, even brought him comics to read

230. in bed. This was real style! Then he dressed in his best suit and went down to meet his mother, who arrived, with his sister, Martha, in a hired car. For once, Martha was deferential. She was impressed, and the sight of the chapel impressed her even more. In front of the High Altar there was an isolated prie-dieu for Denis himself, and behind him a special pew was reserved for her and

235. his mother.

Denis knew afterwards that he hadn't made a single false move. Only once was his exaltation disturbed, and that was when he heard the *ping* of a slingshot and realised that Stein, sitting by himself in the back row, was whiling away the time by getting into fresh mischief. The rage rose up in

240. Denis, in spite of all his holy thoughts, and for a moment he resolved that when it was all over he would find Willy Stein and beat him to a jelly.

Instead, when it was over he suddenly felt weary. Martha had ceased to be impressed by him. Now she was just a sister a bare year younger who was mad with him for having stolen the attention of everybody. She knew only too well

245. what a figure she would have cut as a convert, and was crazy with jealousy.

'I won't stand it,' she said. 'I'm going to be a Catholic, too.'

'Well, who's stopping you?' Denis asked.

'Nobody's going to stop me,' said Martha. 'Just because Daddy is fond of you doesn't mean that I can't be a Catholic.'

250. 'What has Daddy to do with it?' asked Denis with a feeling of alarm.

'Because now that you're a Catholic, the courts wouldn't let him have you,' Martha said excitedly. 'Because Daddy is an atheist, or something, and he wanted to get hold of you. He tried to get you away from Mummy. I don't care about Daddy. I'm going to be converted, too.'

255. 'Go on!' growled Denis, feeling sadly how his mood of exaltation was fading. 'You're only an old copycat.'

'I am not a copycat, Denis Halligan,' she said bitterly, 'It's only that you always sucked up to Daddy and I didn't, and he doesn't care about me. I don't care about him, either, so there!'

260. Denis felt a sudden pang of terror at her words. In a dim sort of way he realized that what he had done might have consequences he had never contemplated. He had no wish to live with his father, but his father came to the school to see him sometimes, and he had always had the feeling that if he ever got fed up with living at home with his mother and Martha, his father would

265. always have him. Nobody had told him that by becoming a Catholic he had

made it impossible for his father to have him. He glanced round and saw Stein, thin and pale and furtive, slouching away from the chapel with his hand in his pocket clutching his slingshot. He gave Denis a grin in which there was no malice, but Denis scowled and looked away.

270.   'Who's that?' asked Martha inquisitively.

'Oh him!' Denis said contemptuously. 'That's only a dirty Jew-boy.'

Yet even as he spoke the words he knew they were false. What he really felt towards Willy Stein was an aching envy. Nobody had told him that by changing his faith he might be unfaithful to his father, but nobody had told

275. Stein, either, and, alone and despairing, he still clung to a faith that was not his own for the sake of a father and mother he had already almost forgotten, who had been murdered half a world away and whom he would never see again. For a single moment Denis saw the dirty little delinquent whom everyone pitied and despised transfigured by a glory that he himself would

280. never know.

A Minority by Frank O'Connor

1. Read lines 1 to 38 ('Nigel only gave a superior sniff').

(a) Why are Willy and Denis not with the rest of the boys in the chapel?
(2)

(b) Explain, in your own words, why Willy Stein is living in Ireland.   (4)

(c) Why do you think Denis is so interested in Willy?   (2)

2. (a) Nigel says, 'You'd want to mind yourself with him' (line 50). Why does he give this advice to Denis?   (4)

(b) Why does Denis pay no attention to Nigel's advice?   (2)

3. Read lines 97 to 163 ('The two boys went into chapel ... ... attention to your lessons')

(a) Willy and Denis differ in their attitude towards religion. In what ways?
(3)

(b) What are Denis's reasons for wishing to become a Catholic and what are his reactions when his mother agrees to it?   (4)

4. Read lines 164 to 194 ('Yet the moment he had made his decision .... it never did him any good at all.')

Explain, in your own words, why Denis wants Willy to become a Catholic too and say why his efforts are unsuccessful.   (8)

5. When Denis learns that Willy is a Jew, what effect does it have on him?
(3)

6. Denis, at first, was excited about 'his own reception into the Church' (line 227). Later, however, we are told that, 'When it was over he suddenly felt weary' (line 242). Explain his change of mood.   (4)

7. In the final paragraph it says, 'What he really felt towards Willy Stein was an aching envy.' Explain what you think this means.   (4)

40 Marks

Paper 2, Comprehension B

Read the article and study the advertisements below. Then answer the questions which follow.

Children and Money by Maryon Tysoe (New Society, 15 December, 1983)

'I'm saving,' said six year old David without a suspicion of a smirk, 'to go to the North Pole. I've got £1.08p in my money box.'
5. Then there's Jamie, seven: 'I'm saving for so I can scare people. I'll get a pump kin and put it on my head and frighten people when they go shopping.'
10. His classmate, Alan, six, is a touch more altruistic. When I ask him what he spends his pocket money on, he says: 'I don't spend it. I save up and buy people
15. presents at Christmas.'
Children and their pocket money are one of those fascinating topics that people rarely seem to discuss. But according to the
20. Wall's 1983 pocket money survey, Britain's ten million five-to-16 year olds were given almost £640 million in pocket money this year. Children between five and seven
25. get on average 71p a week; from eight to ten, 105p; and from eleven to 13, 130p. Not bad, really.
And what do they spend it on? A 1982 marketing survey by
30. Carrick James revealed that the money of children between seven and twelve 'is mainly spent on confectionery, snacks and ice cream.' They give a nauseating,
35. gooey list of the top favourites: in order, sweets, crisps/savoury snacks, chewing/bubble gum, chocolate bars, ice cream and soft drinks. Our children's teeth must
40. be decaying at a rate of knots.
Children also, of course, spend on comics, toys, games and dolls. A recent issue of Moneycare, the NatWest customer magazine,
45. says: 'Electronic toys are a hundred million pound boom business now. But Britain's children are still plumping for good old furry animals, plastic toys, dyecast
50. metal bits and pieces, and anything on wheels.' Useful hints for Christmas presents.
I went to visit two primary schools in north London, and
55. talked to over 70 children about their pocket money. In one school—let's call it 'Orange'— most of the children I spoke to were 'working class' (according to
60. the Registrar General, anyway)

with a sprinkling of 'middles.' At the other school ('Yellow') it was the reverse. So 'school ethos' was inextricably mixed-up with social
65. class. But my straw poll found signs that some class differences in monetary practices may have begun to fade.
Two earlier studies show how
70. things used to be. In 1976, John and Elizabeth Newson, child psychologists at Nottingham University, published a major study of more than 700 seven year
75. olds. They found that working class children got more pocket money than middle class children, and saved less. They say: 'Having cash in hand is equated with en-
80. joying the good life: the relationship between money and enjoyment is specific and direct. . .The working class child already begins to fall into this traditional
85. pattern of life in his use of pocket money.' The middle classes, on the other hand, were prone to saving and 'postponed pleasure.'
Even in 1981, the pattern
90. seemed to persist. Paul Webley, who is lecturer in psychology at Exeter University, says, 'We set up scenarios and said, What would you do with 20p?' The middle
95. class children say they will save. Even when we say 'You have stolen it from your mother's purse,' 50 per cent said they would save it! But the working class
100. children very sensibly said they would rush out and spend it.'
But among the London children I spoke to—mainly six and ten years old—every child but one
105. (out of 73 who got pocket money) said they saved. Over half the six year olds, and half of the ten year olds in each school, said they saved 'sometimes'—the rest either
110. 'usually' or every week. Most children had money boxes: a bewildering array of owls, yellow elephants, frogs, ETs, teddy bears and lots of piggies.
115. The most surprising thing was the number of children with accounts where they deposited their savings: in a bank, building society or the post office. A tiny
120. number of middle class six year

olds already had an account. But among the older children, the 'class gap' seemed to be closing.
In Orange school, I talked to
125. eleven ten year olds about savings accounts. Four out of the nine working class children, and both 'lower middle' children, had an account. In Yellow school, six out
130. of ten middle class ten year olds had one. So did four out of the five working class children in the same form. And another girl confided, 'I'm going to
135. take up a Barclays supersavers— one of those kids' accounts—after Christmas.'
The numbers here are all very small. But a study last year of 444
140. seven to twelve year olds supports the idea that perhaps class differences in children's monetary habits are disappearing. Adrian Furnham and Paul Thomas, both
145. psychologists at University College, London, found no significant class differences over pocket money or saving.
And what are all these children
150. saving *for*? You'll be touched to know that a good few of the children I saw were busily saving for Christmas presents. Jane, seven, from Orange school, told
155. me: 'I'm going to get my grandma a box of chocolates—I've got my grandad an ashtray. I'm getting my mum a cuddly toy, and my grandma's dog, Towzer, a
160. squeaky ball, and my dad a box of hankies.' Martha, six, at Yellow school, said: 'I bought mummy a little white teddy bear, and my sister Chris one of those
165. comb slides to go in your hair, and Jessica—our au pair—a little candle, and daddy a wooden spoon because he's moving. They have a divorce.'
170. A number of children were saving for toys and big items. John (six, Yellow) said with shining honesty: 'Well, my sister is a saver but I'm not a saver. But
175. most of the time I have to put it in my money box, because mum and dad want me to save up for the bank. I want to save up for a Porsche—you know, those posh
180. cars—or a Lotus.' Some children

didn't know quite what they were saving for.

There is evidence that children will have more knowledge of the use of money if they save. And psychologists have paid some attention to the way children's understanding of money and economics develops. Adrian Furnham sums it up like this: 'In the first phase, the child does not understand the role of money in transactions ... It is seen as a right or moral imperative [of the 'You go to jail if you don't' variety], rather than an exchange. In the second phase, the child may understand the nature of the immediate exchange but not the network of exchanges within the monetary system, the divisibility of money [for example, a child with a 20p piece may think he or she cannot buy a littlipop for 10p] or its origin. The third stage involves the understanding of all major types of exchange and hence the concepts of profit, investment, interest.'

Children's developing view of money does have some wonderful hiccups. A recent study in Britain by American psychologist Hans Furth, shows that when children are young, their beliefs about the origins of money can be—literally—fantastic. A six year old

is quoted as saying money comes from 'God. He sent the money, though. Before you were born He sent everything down. Everyone's got it now, in their purses and the men got some in their wallets.' When they are a bit older, they do start to link money with work—and may say things like 'They make it in the Royal Mint.' Some children mention circulation. A six year old said: 'The dustman, he's paid by the government who get the money from the miners who get it from the postmen who get it from the post office who get it from the government.'

What about the concept of profit? Gustav Jahoda, Professor of Psychology at Strathclyde University, has studied 120 working class Glasgow children between six and twelve. He found that young children do not appreciate that shopkeepers have to pay for goods. Then they think shopkeepers buy and sell at the same price. Around the age of eleven, children begin to realise not only that they buy at a lower price than they sell, but also that the profit is used to pay shop assistants and buy more goods.

Certainly a minority of the ten year olds I met seemed to have

cottoned on. When I asked Linda to guess how much a chocolate bar she had just paid 10p for would cost the shopkeeper, she said: 'He would pay about 6p, because he has to make a profit because he works for a living.'

It looks as though London children may be quite economically advanced. The teacher of the sixes and sevens at Yellow school asked his class the 'choc bar' question. He told me: 'One third said less' straight away. And when asked why, they said, Because they have to make money by selling to you.' Some said 10p and some said he made them. A few said more'—but it was wild guessing, because they do not understand the notion of exchange.'

And what of a more advanced concept altogether—banking? Gustav Jahoda has found that Scottish primary school children see banks simply as places to keep money safely, having no idea about borrowing from it or interest. But the fact that banks make profits too will eventually dawn.

To judge by Orange and Yellow schools, we are already breeding a new generation of tiny economic sophisticates.

"New Griffin Savers Account has a lot to offer young savers."

If you're under 17 (and over seven) you'll find our new Griffin Savers Account has a lot to offer and you can open one with just £10.

What's more, the whole sum goes into your account immediately and earns a special rate of interest every six months.

When you open the account we give you a free sports bag, project folder, dictionary, maths set, magazine, and a home bank file so you can keep track of your money. In return all you have to do is keep at least £10 in your account for six months.

So if you're looking for an offer that's too good to refuse, come and talk to us at your local Midland Bank.

A project folder – for collecting your thoughts.

A sports bag – for people who do bags of sport.

A savings book – for paying in and drawing out.

A members card – for members only.

A savings file – for keeping the records straight

A dictionary – so you'll never be lost for words.

A maths set – for working out all the best angles.

Midland Griffin Savers

Only from the Listening Bank

Midland Bank plc

If you are already a Midland saver we will ask you to deposit a further £10 with us to get the Griffin Savers gifts.

Children and Money by Maryon Tysoe

1. David, Jamie and Alan each have different reasons for saving money. Say what these differences are. (3)

2. Read lines 16 to 52. In these lines the writer gives facts *and* personal comments. Quote *THREE* facts and *THREE* personal comments. (6)

3. According to the studies carried out in 1976 and 1981, what was the pattern of children's money habits in the past? (4)

4. According to the writer's own investigation, how have children's money habits changed? What *OTHER* evidence does the writer offer to support her findings? (4)

5. Read the 2 paragraphs, the first of which begins 'And what are all these children saving *for*?' and the second of which begins 'A number of children were saving for toys and big items.'

What light do these children's comments throw on their personal circumstances and family life? (3)

6. Summarise the ideas and misconceptions children have about money. (10)

7. Study the advertisements for Griffin Midland Savers and the NATWEST Piggy Bankers.

(a) What similarities and what differences are there in the two banks' methods of persuading children to save? (5)

(b) Which bank has the scheme which, in your opinion, would probably be most successful in encouraging children to save? Explain why. (5)

40 Marks

Acknowledgements

The authors and publishers wish to thank the following for permission to reprint copyright material:

Alan Paton and Jonathan Cape Ltd. for the story 'Ha'penny' from *Debbie Go Home*; Sid Chaplin and the Longman Group Ltd. for 'The Berry Holly' from *Loves, Hopes and Fears*; Peter Waymark for 'Hologram holidays and calls to the cooker', *The Times*, 7th January, 1984; The Estate of the late Sonia Brownell Orwell and Martin Secker and Warburg Ltd. for extracts from *The Road to Wigan Pier*; Exley Publications Ltd. for extracts from *Grandmas and Grandpas*, ed. by Richard and Helen Exley; A.D.Peters and Co. Ltd., for 'Their Mother's Purse' from *Short Stories* by Morley Callaghan and 'A Minority' from *Collection Three* by Frank O'Connor; Susan Tirbutt for 'All they are saying is give peace a chance', *The Guardian*, 3rd January, 1984; Paul Brown for 'A generation on the main line to tragedy', *The Guardian*, 3rd January, 1984; Doris Lessing and Jonathan Clowes Ltd., London, for 'A Sunrise on the Veldt' from *This was the Old Chief's Country*; Stephen Young for 'Flight path to a good tip', *The Guardian*, 22nd March, 1984; *The Lancashire Evening Post* for 'Lapwing feathers a nest on jet runway', 1st June, 1984; Chatto and Windus and the Wilfred Owen Estate for 'Dulce et Decorum Est'; Arthur Marwick and Macmillan Publishers Ltd. for the extract from *The Deluge: British Society and the First World War*; John Ray and Pergamon Press for the extract from *A History of Britain 1900—1939*; Trevor Fishlock for 'Star Wallahs in the Ascendancy', *The Times*, 13th January, 1983; Karl Sabbagh for 'Stars Shine in Your Eyes', *The Listener*, 24th February, 1983; Professor Alan Smithers for 'Do the stars shape our destinies', *The Guardian*, 19th March, 1984; Polly Toynbee for 'A Hell of a Hotel', *The Guardian*, 5th March, 1984; The Estate of H.E. Bates and Laurence Pollinger Ltd. for 'It's Just the Way it is' from *The Stories of Flying Officer X*; Maryon Tysoe for 'Children and Money', *New Society*, 15th December, 1983.

The Blood Donor recruitment advertisement (p. 64) and the table on Young People and Crime (p. 94) are reproduced with the permission of the Controller of Her Majesty's Stationery Office; The NSPCC, Christian Aid and The Cancer Research Campaign advertisements are reproduced by courtesy of those charities; The Forest Holidays advertisement is reproduced by courtesy of the Forestry Commission. The advertisements for the NATWEST Piggy Bank and MIDLAND Griffin Savers are reproduced by courtesy of the MIDLAND and NATIONAL WESTMINSTER banks.

It has not been possible in all cases to trace copyright holders; the publishers would be glad to hear from any such unacknowledged copyright holders.

The authors would especially like to thank the following people for their assistance in the writing of this book: Karen Lloyd, Valerie Pound, Carol Lewis, Sheree Jones, David Smith, Maria Cross, David Howarth, Jayne McGrath, Gillian Kirkpatrick, Tracey Coe, Chris Damp, Margaret Murphy, Mrs E. Paterson, Mr. W. Fisher and his grandchildren.